Father Ryan's Poems

By

Abram Joseph Ryan

Published by Forgotten Books 2012
Originally Published 1879

PIBN 1000425946

FATHER RYANS
POEMS.

"All Rests with those who Read. A work or thought
Is what each makes it to himself, and may
Be full of great dark meanings, like the sea,
With shoals of life rushing; or like the air,
Benighted with the wing of the wild dove,
Sweeping miles broad o'er the far southern woods,
With mighty glimpses of the central light,—
Or may be nothing—bodiless, spiritless."
                              —FESTUS.

MOBILE:

JNO. L. RAPIER & CO., PUBLISHERS.

1879.

These

Simple Rhymes

Are Laid as a Garland of Love

At the Feet of His Mother By

Her Child, The

Author.

THESE VERSES (which some friends call by the higher title of Poems—to which appellation the Author objects),—were written at random,—off and on,—here,—there,—any-where,—just when the mood came, with little of study and less of art,—and always in a hurry.

Hence they are incomplete in finish, as the Author is;—tho' he thinks they are true in tone. His feet know more of the humble steps that lead up to the Altar and its Mysteries, than of the steeps that lead up to Parnassus and the Home of the Muses. And souls were always more to him than songs. But still somehow,—and he could not tell why,—he sometimes tried to sing. Here are his simple songs. He never dreamed of taking even lowest place in the rank of authors. But friends persisted; and finally a young lawyer friend, who has entire charge of his business in the book, forced him to front the world and its critics. There are verses connected with the war published in this volume not for harm-sake, nor for hate-sake, but simply because the Author wrote them. He would write again in the same tone and key under the same circumstances. No more need be said, except that these verses mirror the mind of

THE AUTHOR.

CONTENTS.

CONTENTS.

CONTENTS.

SONG OF THE MYSTIC.

I WALK down the Valley of Silence,—
　　Down the dim, voiceless valley alone!
And I hear not the fall of a footstep
　　Around me save God's and my own;
And the hush of my heart is as holy
　　As hovers where angels have flown!

Long ago—was I weary of voices
　　Whose music my heart could not win;
Long ago I was weary of noises
　　That fretted my soul with their din;
Long ago was I weary of places
　　Where I met but the human—and sin.

I walked in the world with the worldly;
　　I craved what the world never gave;
And I said: "In the world each Ideal,
　　That shines like a star on life's wave;
Is wrecked on the shores of the Real,
　　And sleeps like a dream in a grave."

And still did I pine for the Perfect,
　　And still found the False with the True;
I sought 'mid the Human for Heaven,
　　But caught a mere glimpse of its Blue:
And I wept when the clouds of the mortal
　　Veiled even that glimpse from my view.

And I toiled on heart-tired of the Human;
  And I moaned 'mid the mazes of men;
Till I knelt long ago at an altar
  And heard a voice call me:—since then
I walk down the Valley of Silence
  That lies far beyond mortal ken.

Do you ask what I found in the Valley?
  'Tis my Trysting Place with the Divine.
And I fell at the feet of the Holy,
  And above me a voice said: "Be mine."
And there arose from the depths of my spirit
  An echo—"My heart shall be thine."

Do you ask how I live in the Valley?
  I weep—and I dream—and I pray.
But my tears are as sweet as the dewdrops
  That fall on the roses in May;
And my prayer, like a perfume from Censers,
  Ascendeth to God night and day.

In the hush of the Valley of Silence
  I dream all the songs that I sing;
And the music floats down the dim Valley,
  Till each finds a word for a wing,
That to hearts, like the Dove of the Deluge,
  A message of Peace they may bring.

But far on the deep there are billows
  That never shall break on the beach;
And I have heard songs in the Silence
  That never shall float into speech;
And I have had dreams in the Valley
  Too lofty for language to reach.

And I have seen Thoughts in the Valley,—
    Ah me! how my spirit was stirred!
And they wear holy veils on their faces,—
    Their footsteps can scarcely be heard:
They pass through the Valley, like Virgins
    Too pure for the touch of a word!

Do you ask me the place of the Valley?
    Ye hearts that are harrowed by Care!
It lieth afar between mountains
    And God and his angels are there:
And one is the dark mount of Sorrow,
    And one,—the bright mountain of Prayer!

LIFE.

BABY played with the surplice sleeve
    Of a gentle priest; while in accents low
The sponsors murmured the grand "I believe."
    And the priest bade the mystic waters flow,
In the name of the Father, and the Son,
And Holy Spirit—Three in One.

    Spotless as a lily's leaf,
        Whiter than the Christmas snow;
    Not a sign of sin or grief,
        And the babe laughed sweet and low.

A smile flitted over the baby's face:
  Or was it the gleam of its angel's wing
Just passing then, and leaving a trace
  Of its presence, as it soared to sing?
A hymn when words and waters win
To Grace and life—a child of sin.

  Not an outward sign or token,
    That a child was saved from woe,
  But the bonds of sin were broken;
    And the babe laughed sweet and ow.

A cloud rose up to the mother's eyes,—
  And out of the cloud grief's rain fell fast,
Came the baby's smiles, and the mother's sighs,
  Out of the future, or the past?—
Ah! gleam and gloom must ever meet,
  And gall must mingle with the sweet.

  Yea, upon the baby's laughter
    Trickled tears: 'tis ever so—·
  Mothers dread the dark hereafter;
    But the babe laughed sweet and low.

And the years like waves broke on the shore
  Of the mother's heart, and her baby's life;
But her lone heart drifted away before
  Her little boy knew an hour of strife;—
Drifted away on a Summer's eve,
  Ere the orphaned child knew how to grieve.

  Her humble grave was gently made,
    Where roses bloomed in Summer's glow;
  The wild birds sang where her heart was laid;
    And her boy laughed sweet and low,

He drifted away from his mother's grave
   Like a fragile flower on a great stream's tide.
'Till he heard the moan of the mighty wave,
   That welcomed the stream to the ocean wide.
Out from the shore and over the deep,—
   He sailed away and learned to weep.

     Furrowed grew the face once fair,
      Under storms of human woe;—
     Silvered grew the dark brown hair,
      And he wailed so sad and low.

The years swept on as erst they swept,
   Bright wavelets once—dark billows now.
Wherever he sailed—he ever wept,
   A cloud hung over the darkened brow—·
Over the deep and into the dark,
   But no one knew where sank his bark.

     Wild roses watched his mother's tomb,
      The world still laughed, 'tis ever so,—
     God only knows the baby's doom,
      That laughed so sweet and low.

MARCH OF THE DEATHLESS DEAD.

ATHER the sacred dust
   Of the warriors tried and true,
Who bore the flag of our People's trust
   And fell in a cause, though lost still just
     And died for me and you.

Gather them one and all!
　From the Private to the Chief,
Come they from hovel or princely hall,
They fell for us, and for them should fall
　The tears of a Nation's grief.

Gather the corpses strewn
　O'er many a battle plain;
From many a grave that lies so lone,
Without a name and without a stone,
　Gather the Southern slain.

We care not whence they came,
　Dear in their lifeless clay!
Whether unknown, or known to fame,
Their cause and country still the same—
　They died—and wore the **Gray**.

Wherever the brave have died,
　They should not rest apart;
Living they struggled side by side—
Why should the hand of Death divide
　A single heart from heart.

Gather their scattered clay,
　Wherever it may rest;
Just as they marched to the bloody fray;
Just as they fell on the battle day;
　Bury them breast to breast.

The foeman need not dread
　This gathering of the brave;
Without sword or flag, and with soundless **tread,**
We muster once more our deathless dead;
　Out of each lonely grave.

The foeman need not frown,
    They all are powerless now—
We gather them here and we lay them down,
And tears and prayers are the only crown
    We bring to wreathe each brow.

And the dead thus meet the dead,
    While the living o'er them weep;
And the men by Lee and Stonewall led,
And the hearts that once together bled,
    Together still shall sleep.

LAST OF MAY.

TO THE CHILDREN OF MARY OF THE CATHEDRAL OF MOBILE.

IN the mystical Dim of the Temple,—
    In the dream-haunted Dim of the Day,—
The Sunlight spoke soft to the Shadows,
    And said: "With my gold and your gray,
Let us meet at the shrine of the Virgin,—
    And ere her fair Feast pass away
Let us weave there a mantle of glory
    To deck the Last Evening of May.

The tapers were lit on the altar
    With garlands of lilies between;
And the steps leading up to the statue
    Flashed bright with the roses' red sheen;
The sungleams came down from the Heavens
    Like angels, to hallow the scene,
And they seemed to kneel down with the shadows
    That crept to the shrine of the Queen.

The singers,—their hearts in their voices,
    Had chanted the anthems of old;
And the last trembling wave of the Vespers
    On the far-shores of silence had rolled.
And there,—at the Queen-Virgin's altar
    The Sun wove the mantle of gold
While the hands of the Twilight were weaving
    A fringe for the flash of each fold.

And wavelessly, in the deep silence,
    Three banners hung peaceful and low,—
They bore the bright Blue of the Heavens
    They wore the pure White of the snow,—
And beneath them fair children were kneeling,
    Whose faces, with graces aglow,
Seemed sinless,—in land that is sinful
    And woeless,—in life full of woe.

Their heads wore the veil of the lily,—
    Their brows wore the wreath of the rose,
And their hearts, like their flutterless banners,
    Were stilled in a holy repose.
Their shadowless eyes were uplifted,
    Whose glad gaze would never disclose
That from eyes that are most like the Heavens
    The dark rain of tears soonest flows.

The Banners were borne to the railing
    Beneath them—a group from each band,—
And they bent their bright folds for the Blessing
    That fell from the Priest's lifted hand.
And he signed the three, fair, silken standards,
    With a Sign never foe could withstand,—
What stirred them? The breeze of the Evening?
    Or a breath from the far-Angel-land?

Then came, two by two, to the altar,
  The young and the pure and the fair,—
Their faces the mirror of Heaven,—
  Their hands folded meekly in prayer,
They came for a simple blue ribbon
  For love of Christ's mother to wear,—
And I believe, with the children of Mary
  The Angels of Mary were there.

Ah! Faith! simple Faith of the children!
  You still shame the Faith of the old!
Ah! love! simple love of the Little!
  You still warm the love of the cold!
And the Beautiful God who is wandering
  Far out in the world's dreary wold,
Finds a Home in the Hearts of the children
  And a Rest with the Lambs of the Fold.

Swept a voice ;—was it wafted from Heaven?
  Heard you ever the Sea when its sings,
Where it sleeps on the shore in the Night-time?
  Heard you ever the hymns the breeze brings,
From the hearts of a thousand bright summers?
  Heard you ever the bird, when she springs
To the clouds, till she seems to be only
  A song of a shadow on wings?

Came a voice,—and an "Ave Maria"
  Rose out of a heart rapture-thrilled
And in the embrace of its music
  The souls of a thousand lay stilled.
A voice with the tones of an angel,
  Never flower such a sweetness distilled ;
It faded away,—but the temple
  With its perfume of worship was nlled.

Then back to the Queen-Virgin's altar
  The white veils swept on two by two;—
And the holiest halo of heaven
  Flashed out from the ribbons of Blue;—
And they laid down the wreaths of the roses
  Whose hearts were as pure as their hue,—
Ah! they to the Christ are the truest,
  Whose loves to the Mother are true!

And thus in the Dim of the Temple
  In the dream-haunted Dim of the Day,–
The Angels and Children of Mary
  Met ere their Queen's Feast passed away,
Where the Sungleams knelt down with the Shadows
  And wove with their gold and their gray   .
A mantle of grace and of glory
  For the Last, lovely Evening of May.

THE SWORD OF ROBERT LEE.

ORTH from its scabbard pure and bright,
  Flashed the sword of Lee!
Far in the front of the deadly fight
High o'er the brave in the cause of Right
Its stainless sheen like a beacon light
  Led us to Victory.

Out of its scabbard where full long
  It slumbered peacefully,—
Roused from its rest by the battle's song
Shielding the feeble, smiting the strong
Guarding the right, avenging the wrong
  Gleamed the sword of Lee.

Forth from its scabbard high in air
  Beneath Virginia's sky—
And they who saw it gleaming there
And knew who bore it knelt to swear,
That where that sword led, they would dare
  To follow and to die.

Out of its scabbard!—never hand
  Waved sword from stain as free,
Nor purer sword led braver band,
Nor braver bled for a brighter land,
Nor brighter land had a Cause so grand,
  Nor cause a chief like Lee.

Forth from its scabbard! how we prayed,
  That sword might victor be;—
And when our triumph was delayed,
And many a heart grew sore afraid,
We still hoped on while gleamed the blade
  Of noble Robert Lee.

Forth from its scabbard! all in vain
  Bright flashed the sword of Lee;—
'Tis shrouded now in its sheath again,
It sleeps the sleep of our noble slain;
Defeated yet without a stain,
  Proudly and peacefully.

AT LAST.

INTO a temple vast and dim,
  Solemn and vast and dim,
Just when the last sweet Vesper Hymn
  Was floating far away—
With eyes that tabernacled tears—
  Her heart the home of tears—
And cheeks wan with the woes of years,
  A woman went one day.

And, one by one, adown the aisles—
  Adown the long, lone aisles—
Their faces bright with holy smiles
  That follow after Prayer—
The worshipers in silence passed—
  In silence slowly passed away;
The woman knelt until the last
  Had left her lonely there.

A holy hush came o'er the place—
  O'er the holy place—
The shadows kissed her woe-worn face,
  Her forehead touched the floor;
The wreck that drifted thro' the years—
  Sin-driven thro' the years—
Was floating o'er the tide of tears,
  To mercy's golden shore.

Her lips were sealed, they could not pray—
    They sighed, but could not pray—
All words of Prayer had died away
    From them long years ago;
But ah! from out her eyes there rose—
    Sad from her eyes there rose—
The prayer of tears, which swiftest goes
    To Heaven—winged with woe.

With weary tears, her weary eyes—
    Her joyless, weary eyes—
Wailed forth a Rosary—and her sighs
    And sobs strung all the Beads;
The while before her spirit's gaze—
    Her contrite spirit's gaze—
Moved all the mysteries of her days
    And histories of her deeds.

Still as a shadow, while she wept—
    So desolately wept—
Up thro' the long, lone aisle she crept
    Unto an altar fair;
Mother!"—her pale lips said no more—
    Could say no more—
The wreck, at last, reached Mercy's shore—
    For Mary's shrine was there.

IN MEMORY OF VERY REV. J. B. ETIENNE,

SUPERIOR GENERAL OF THE CONGREGATION OF THE MISSIO?
AND OF THE SISTERS OF CHARITY.

SHADOW slept folded in vestments
   The dream of a smile on its face,
Dim—soft as the gleam after sunset,
   That hangs like a halo of grace,
Where the daylight hath died in the valley,
   And the twilight hath taken its place,
A Shadow! but still on the mortal,
   There rested the tremulous trace
Of the joy of a spirit immortal,
   Passed up to its God in His grace.

A Shadow! hast seen in the summer
   A cloud wear the smile of the sun?
On the shadow of death there is flashing
   The glory of noble deeds done;
On the face of the dead there is glowing
   The light of a holy race run;
And the smile of the face is reflecting
   The gleam of the crown he has won.
Still, Shadow! sleep on in the vestments
   Unstained by the Priest who has gone.

And thro' all the nations, the children
   Of Vincent de Paul wail his loss;
But the glory that crowns him in heaven
   Illumines the gloom of their cross.

They send to the Shadow the tribute
  Of tears, from the fountains of love,
And they send from their altars sweet prayers
  To the throne of their Father above.

Yea! sorrow weeps over the Shadow,
  But Faith looks aloft to the skies;
And Hope, like a rainbow, is flashing
  O'er the tears that rain down from their eyes.
They murmur on earth " De profundis,"
  The low chant is mingled with sighs;
Laudate" rings out through the heavens,
  The dead Priest hath won his faith's prize.

His children in sorrow will honor
  His grave;—every tear is a gem,
And their prayers 'round his brow in the heavens
  Will brighten his fair diadem,—
I kneel at his grave and remember
  In love, I am *still* one of them.

A MEMORY.

ONE bright memory shines like a star
    In the sky of my spirit forever;
  And over my pathway it flashes afar
    A radiance that perishes never.

One bright memory—only one;
  And I walk by the light of its gleaming;
It brightens my days—and when days are done
  It shines in the night o'er my dreaming.

One bright memory—whose golden rays
    Illumine the gloom of my sorrows,
And I know that its lustre will gladden my gaze
    In the shadows of all my to-morrows.

One bright memory—whe . I am sad
    I lift up my eyes to its shining,
And the clouds pass away; and my spirit grows glad
    And my heart hushes all its repining.

One bright memory—others have passed
    Back into the shadows forever;
But it, far and fair, bright and true to the last,
    Sheds a light that will pass away never.

Shine on, shine always, Thou star of my days!
    And when Death's starless Night gathers o'er me,
Beam brighter than ever adown on my gaze,
    And light the dark valley before me.

THE PRAYER OF THE SOUTH.

Y BROW is bent beneath a heavy rod!
    My face is wan and white with many woes,
But I will lift my poor chained hands to God,
    And for my children pray, and for my foes.
Beside the graves where thousands lowly lie
    I kneel, and weeping for each slaughtered son,
I turn my gaze to my own sunny sky,
    And pray, oh! Father, Let Thy will be done!

My heart is filled with anguish, deep and vast;
   My hopes are buried with my children's dust;
My joys have fled, my tears are flowing fast—
   In whom, save Thee, our Father, shall I trust?
Ah! I forgot The,   her, long and oft,
   When I was happy, rich, and proud, and free;
But conquered now, and crushed, I look aloft,
   And sorrow leads me, Father, back to thee.

Amid the wrecks that mark the foeman's path
   I kneel, and wailing o'er my glories gone,
I still each thought of hate, each throb of wrath,
   And whisper, Father, let thy will be done!
Pity me, Father of the Desolate!
   Alas! my burdens are so hard to bear;
Look down in mercy on my wretched fate,
   And keep me, guard me, with thy loving care.

Pity me, Father, for His holy sake,
   Whose broken heart bled at the feet of grief,
That hearts of earth, wherever they shall break,
   Might go to His and find a sure relief.
Ah, me, how dark!   Is this a brief eclipse?
   Or is it night with no morrow's sun?
Oh! Father! Father! with my pale, sad lips,
   And sadder heart, I pray, Thy will be done.

My homes are joyless, and a million mourn
   Where many met in joys forever flown;
Whose hearts were light, are burdened now and **torn;**
   Where many smiled, but one is left to moan.
And, ah! the widow's wails, the orphan's cries,
   Are morning hymn and vesper chant to me;
And groans of men and sounds of women's sighs
   Commingle, Father, with my prayer to Thee.

Beneath my feet ten thousand children dead—
   Oh! how I loved each known and nameless one!
Above their dust I bow my crownless head,
   And murmur—Father, still Thy will be done.
Ah! Father, Thou didst deck my own loved land
   With all bright charms, and beautiful and fair;
But foemen came, and, with a ruthless hand,
   Spread ruin, wreck and desolation there.

Girdled with gloom, of all my brightness shorn,
   And garmented with grief, I kiss Thy rod,
And turn my face, with tears all wet and worn,
   To catch one smile of pity from my God.
Around me blight, where all before was bloom,
   And so much lost, alas! and nothing won!
Save this—that I can lean on wreck and tomb,
   And weep, and weeping, pray, Thy will be done.

And oh! 'tis hard to say, but said, 'tis sweet;
   The words are bitter, but they hold a balm—
A balm that heals the wounds of my defeat,
   And lulls my sorrows into holy calm.
It is the prayer of prayers, and how it brings,
   When heard in Heaven, peace and hope to me!
When Jesus prayed it, did not angels' wings
   Gleam 'mid the darkness of Gethsemane?

My children, Father, Thy forgiveness need;
   Alas! their hearts have only place for tears!
Forgive them, Father, ev'ry wrongful deed
   And ev'ry sin of those four bloody years,
And give them strength to bear their boundless loss,
   And from their hearts take every thought of hate;
And while they climb their Calvary with their Cross,
   Oh! help them, Father, to endure its weight.

And for my dead, my Father, may I pray?
   Ah! sighs may soothe, but prayer shall soothe me more!
I keep eternal watch above their clay;
   Oh! rest their souls, my Father, I implore!
Forgive my foes—they know not what they do—
   Forgive them all the tears they made me shed;
Forgive them, though my noblest sons they slew,
   And bless them, though they curse my poor, dear dead.

Oh! may my woes be each a carrier-dove,
   With swift, white wings, that, bathing in my tears,
Will bear Thee, Father, all my prayers of love,
   And bring me peace in all my doubts and fears.
Father, I kneel, 'mid ruin, wreck and grave—
   A desert waste, where all was erst so fair—
And for my children and my foes I crave
   Pity and Pardon—Father, hear my prayer!

A MEMORY.

DOWN the valley dripped a stream,
   White lilies drooped on either side;
Our hearts, in spite of us, will dream
   In such a place, at Eventide.

   Bright wavelets wove the scarf of Blue
     That well became the valley fair,—
   And grassy fringe of greenest hue
     Hung round its borders everywhere.

And where the stream, in wayward whirls
  Went winding in and winding out,
Lay shells that wore the look of pearls
  Without their pride, all strewn about

And here and there along the strand,
  Where some ambitious wave had strayed,
Rose little monuments of sand
  As frail as those by mortals made.

And many a flower was blooming there
  In beauty, yet without a name,
Like humble hearts that often bear
  The gifts,—but not the palm of fame.

The rainbow's tints could never vie
  With all the colors that they wore;
While bluer than the bluest sky,
  The stream flowed on 'tween shore and shore.

And on the height, and down the side,
  Of either hill that hid the place,
Rose elms in all the stately pride
  Of youthful strength and ancient race.

While here and there the trees between,—
  Bearing the scars of battle-shocks,
And frowning wrathful, might be seen
  The moss-veiled faces of the rocks.

And round the rocks crept flowered vines
  And clomb the trees that towered high,—
The type of a lofty thought that twines
  Around a Truth, to touch the sky.

And to that vale from first of May
    Until the last of August went;—
Beauty, the exile, came each day
    In all her charms, to cast her tent.

'Twas there, one long-gone August day
    I wandered down the valley fair,—
The spell has never passed away
    That fell upon my spirit there.

The summer sunset glorified
    The clouded face of dying day
Which flung a smile upon the tide
    And lilies, ere he passed away.

And o'er the valley's grassy slopes
    There fell an evanescent sheen,
That flashed and faded like the hopes
    That haunt us, of what might have been.

And rock and tree flung back the light
    Of all the sunset's golden gems,
As if it were beneath their right
    To wear such borrowed diadems.

Low in the west gleam after gleam,
    Glowed faint and fainter,—till the last
Made the dying Day a living Dream
    To last as long as life shall last.

And in the arches of the trees
    The wild birds slept with folded wing,
And e'en the lips of the summer-breeze,
    That sang all day, had ceased to sing,

And all was silent,—save the rill
 That rippled round the lilies' feet,—
And sang,—while stillness grew more still
 To listen to the murmur sweet.

And now and then it surely seemed
 The little stream was laughing low,—
As if its sleepy wavelets dreamed
 Such dreams as only children know.

So still,—that not the faintest breath
 Did stir the shadows in the air ;—
It would have seemed the home of Death
 Had I not felt Life sleeping there.

And slow and soft,—and soft and slow
 From darkling earth and darkened sky,
Wide wings of Gloom waved to and fro
 And spectral shadows flitted by.

And then methought upon the sward
 I saw,—or was it starlight's ray ?
Or Angels come to watch and guard
 The valley,—till the dawn of day?

Is every lower life the ward
 Of spirits more divinely wrought?
'Tis sweet to believe 'tis God's,—and hard
 To think 'tis but a Poet's thought.

But God's or Poet's thought,—I ween
 My senses did not fail me when
I saw veiled angels watch that scene
 And guard its sleep,—as they guard men.

A MEMORY.

Sweet sang the stream as on it pressed
    As sorrow sings a heart to sleep,—
As a Mother sings one child to rest
    And for the dead one still will weep.

I walked adown the singing stream,
    The lilies slept on either side ;—
My heart,—it could not help but dream
    At Eve, and after Eventide,

Ah ! dreams of such a lofty reach
    With more than earthly fancies fraught,—
That not the strongest wings of speech
    Could ever touch their lowest thought.

Dreams of the Bright—the Fair,—the Far,
    Heart-fancies flashing Heaven's hue,—
That swept around,—as sweeps a star
    The boundless orbit of the True.

Yea ! dreams all free from earthly taint—
    Where human Passion played no part,—
As pure as thoughts that thrill a Saint
    Or haunt an Archangelic heart.

Ah ! dreams that did not rise from Sense
    And rose too high to stoop to it,—
And flamed aloft like frankincense
    In censers round the Infinite.

Yea ! dreams that vied with Angel's flight
    And soaring,—bore my heart away,—
Beyond the far Star-bounds of Night
    Unto the Everlasting Day.

A MEMORY.

How long I strolled beside the stream
    I do not know, nor may I say ;
But when the Poet ceased to dream
    The Priest went on his knees to pray.

I felt,—as sure a seraph feels,
    When in some golden hour of grace
God smiles,—and suddenly reveals
    A new, strange Glory in His Face.

Ah ! star-lit valley !   Lilies white !
    The Poet dreamed,—ye slumbered deep!
But when the Priest knelt down that Night
    And prayed,—why woke ye from your sleep?

*   *   *   *   *   *
*   *   *   *   *   *
*   *   *   *   *   *

The stream sang down the valley fair—
    I saw the wakened lilies nod,—
I knew they heard me whisper there
    " How beautiful ! art thou, my God ! "

RHYME.

ONE idle day
A mile or so of sunlit waves off shore,
 In a breezeless bay,—
 We listless lay
Our boat a "dream of rest" on the still sea—
 And—we were four.

 The wind had died
That all day long sang songs unto the deep;
 It was eventide—
 And far and wide
Sweet silence crept thro' the rifts of sound
  With spells of sleep.

 Our gray sail cast
The only cloud that flecked the foamless sea,
 And weary at last
 Beside the mast
One fell to slumber, with a dreamy face
 And—we were three.

 No ebb! no flow!
No sound! no stir,—in the wide-wondrous calm
 In the sunset's glow
 The shore shelved low
And snow-white,—from far ridges screened with shade
 Of drooping palm.

Our hearts were hushed ;—
All light seemed melting into boundless blue ;
But the west was flushed
Where sunset blushed,
Thro' clouds of roses, when another slept
And,—we were two.

How still the air !
Not e'en a sea-bird o'er us waveward flew
Peace rested there !
Light ! everywhere !
Nay ! Light ! some shadows fell on that fair scene,
And,—we are two ;

Some shadows !   Where !
No matter where ! all shadows are not seen
For clouds of care,
To skies all fair
Will sudden rise as tears to shining eyes
And dim their sheen.

We spake no word
Tho' each I ween did hear the other's soul.
Not a wavelet stirred
And yet we heard,
The loneliest music of the weariest waves
That ever roll.

Yea ! Peace ! you swayed
Your sceptre jeweled with the evening light,
And then you said
"Here falls no shade,—
Here floats no sound, and all the seas and skies
Sleep calm and bright."

Nay, Peace! Not so!
The wildest waves may feel thy sceptre's spell,
And fear to flow,
But to and fro,—
Beyond their reach lone waves on troubled seas
Will sink and swell.

No word e'en yet
Were our eyes speaking while they watched the sky
And in the sunset,
Infinite regret,
Swept sighing from the skies into our souls
I wonder why!

A half hour passed—
'Twas more than half an age ; 'tis ever thus,
Words came at last,
Fluttering and fast
As shadows veiling sunsets in the souls
Of each of us.

The noiseless night
Sped flitting like a ghost where waves of blue
Lost all their light
As lips once bright
Whence smiles have fled ; we or the wavelets sighed
And we were two.

The day had gone—
And on the dim high altar of the Dark
Stars one by one
Far, faintly shone ;
The moonlight trembled like a mother's smile
Upon our bark.

We softly spoke,
The waves seemed listening on the lonely sea
The winds awoke
Our whispers broke
The spell of silence ; and two eyes unclosed
And we were three.

" The breeze blows fair,"
He said ;—" the waking waves set towards the shore ;"
The long brown hair
Of the other there
Who slumbered near the mast with dreamy face
Stirred :—we were four.

That starry night—
A mile or so of shadows from the shore
Two faces bright
With laughter light
Shone on two souls like stars that shine on shrines
And we were four.

Over the reach
Of dazzling waves our boat like wild bird flew
We reached the beach
Nor song—nor speech
Shall ever tell our Sacramental thought,
When,—we were two.

NOCTURNE.

I SIT, to-night, by the firelight,
　　And I look at the glowing flame,
And I see in the bright red flashes
　　A Heart,—a Face and a Name.

How often have I seen pictures
　　Framed in the firelight's blaze,—
Of hearts, of names and of faces,
　　And scenes of remembered days !

How often have I found poems,
　　In the crimson of the coals,
And the swaying flames of the firelight
　　Unrolled such golden scrolls.

And my eyes, they were proud to read them,
　　In letters of living flame,—
But to-night, in the fire, I see only
　　One Heart,—one Face and one Name.

But where are the olden pictures ?
　　And where are the olden dreams ?
Has a change come over my vision ?
　　Or over the fire's bright gleams ?

Not over my vision, surely—
　　My eyes,—they are still the same,
That used to find in the firelight
　　So many a face and name.

Not over the firelight either,
　　No change in the coals or blaze
That flicker and flash as ruddy
　　To-night, as in other days.

But there must be a change—I feel it,—
　To-night; not an old picture came;
The fire's bright flames only painted
　One heart,—one face and one name.

Three pictures? No! only one picture;—
　The Face belongs to the Name,—
And the Name names the Heart, that is throbbing
　Just back of the beautiful flame.

Who said it? I wonder,—"all faces
　Must fade in the light of but one,—
The soul like the earth, may have many
　Horizons,—but only one sun."

Who dreamt it? Did I? If I dreamt it,
　'Tis true,—every name passes by
Save one;—the sun wears many cloudlets
　Of gold,—but has only one sky.

And out of the flames have they faded
　The hearts and the faces of yore?
Have they sunk 'neath the gray of the ashes
　To rise to my vision no more?

Yes, surely, or else I would see them
　To-night, just as bright as of old,—
In the white of the coals' silver flashes,
　In the red of the restless flames' gold,

Do you say I am fickle and faithless?
　Else why are the old pictures gone?
And why should the visions of many
　Melt into the vision of one?

Nay! list to the voice of the Heavens,
 "One Eternal alone reigns above."
Is it true ?—and all else are but idols?
 So the heart can have only one Love.

Only one,—all the rest are but idols,
 That fall from their shrines soon or late,
When the Love that is Lord of the temple,
 Comes with sceptre and crown to the gate.

To be faithless oft means to be faithful,
 To be false often means to be true,—
The vale that loves clouds that are golden,
 Forgets them for skies that are blue.

To forget often means to remember
 What we had forgotton too long,—
The fragrance is not the bright flower,
 The echo is not the sweet song.

Am I dreaming?   No, there is the firelight
 Gaze—I ever so long—all the same
I only can see in its glowing
 A Heart, a Face and a Name.

Farewell ! all ye hearts, names and faces !
 Only ashes now under the blaze,—
Ye never again will smile on me,—
 For I'm touching the end of my days.

And the beautiful fading firelight
 Paints, now, with a pencil of flame,
Three pictures,—yet only one picture
 A Heart, a Face and a Name.

REVERIE.

ONLY a few more years!
   Weary years!
Only a few more tears!
   Bitter tears!
And then—and then—like other men,—
   I cease to wander,—cease to weep,—
   Dim shadows o'er my way shall creep,—
And out of the Day,—and into the Night,—
Into the Dark, and out of the Bright,—
   I go,—and Death shall veil my face,—
   The feet of the years shall fast efface
   My very name, and every trace
I leave on Earth ;—for the stern years tread,—
Tread out the names of the Gone and Dead!
And then,—ah! then; like other men,—
   I close my eyes,—and go to sleep,—
   Only a few, one hour, shall weep,
   Ah! me!—the Grave is dark and deep.

Alas! Alas!—
   How soon we pass!
And ah! we go—
   So far away?—
When go we must,—
From the Light of Life, and the heat of strife,—
To the Peace of Death, and the cold, still Dust,-
   We go—we go—we may not stay,
   We travel the lone, dark, dreary way;—
Out of the Day and into the Night,—
Into the Darkness,—out of the Bright.—

And then ! ah, then ! like other men,
   We close our eyes—and go to sleep—
   We hush our hearts—and go to sleep,—
   Only a few, one hour, shall weep,
   Ah, me ! the Grave is lone and deep!

I saw a flower, at morn, so fair,—
I passed at Eve,—it was not there,—
   I saw a sunbeam, golden, bright,
   I saw a cloud the sunbeam's shroud,—
And I saw Night
   Digging the Grave of Day,—
And Day took off her golden crown,
And flung it sorrowfully down,—
   Ah ! Day ! the Sun's fair Bride !
   At twilight moaned and died.—
And so, alas !—like Day we pass,—
   At Morn we smile !
At Eve we weep—
   At Morn we wake—
In Night we sleep,
   We close our eyes and go to sleep—
   Ah me ! the Grave is still and deep !

But God is sweet,
   My Mother told me so ;—
When I knelt at her feet,—
   Long—so long ago ;—
She clasped my hands in hers,—
Ah me ! that memory stirs'
   My soul's profoundest Deep—
   No wonder that I weep,—
She clasped my hands,—and smiled,
Ah ! then I was a child,—

REVERIE.

I knew not harm,
My Mother's arm
Was flung around me ;—and I felt—
That when I knelt
To listen to my Mother's prayer,—
God was with mother there.
Yea! "God is sweet,"
She told me so ;—
She never told me wrong,
And through my years of woe
Her whispers soft, and sad, and low,
And sweet as Angel's song,—
Have floated—like a dream.

And, ah! to-night I seem
A very child in my old, old place,
Beneath my Mother's blessed face ;
And through each sweet remembered word,
This sweetest undertone is heard :—
My child !—my child !—our God is sweet,
In Life—in Death—kneel at his feet,—
Sweet in gladness—sweet in gloom,
Sweeter still beside the Tomb.—
Why should I wail ?—Why ought I weep?
The Grave,—it is not dark and deep ;—
Why should I sigh ?—Why ought I moan ?
The Grave,—it is not still and lone ;
Our God is sweet,—our Grave is sweet,
We lie there sleeping at his feet,
Where the wicked shall from troubling cease,
And weary hearts shall rest in peace !

THE OLD YEAR AND THE NEW.

HOW swift they go !
    Life's many years,
        With their winds of woe
            And their storms of tears,
        And their darkest of Nights whose shadowy slopes
Are lit with the flashes of starriest hopes,
And their sunshiny days in whose calm heavens loom
The clouds of the tempest—the shadows of the gloom.

        And ah ! we pray
            With a grief so drear,
        That the years may stay
            When their graves are near ;
Tho' the brows of To-morrows be radiant and bright.
With love and with beauty, with life and with light,
The dead hearts of Yesterdays, cold on the bier,
To the hearts that survive them, are evermore dear.

        For the heart so true,
            To each Old Year cleaves ;
        Tho' the hand of the New
            Flowery garlands weave.
But the flowers of the future tho' fragrant and fair
With the Past's withered leaflets may never compare,
For dear is each dead leaf—and dearer each thorn—
In the wreaths which the brows of our Past years have worn

Yea ! men will cling
    With a love to the last ;
And wildly fling
    Their arms round their Past !
As the vine that clings to the oak that falls,
As the ivy twines round the crumbled walls ;
For the dust of the Past some hearts higher prize,
Than the stars that flash out from the Future's bright skies,

And why not so !
    The old, old Years,
They knew and they know
    All our hopes and fears ;
We walked by their side, and we told them each grief,
And they kissed off our tears while they whispered relief
And the stories of hearts that may not be revealed
In the hearts of the dead years are Buried and sealed.

Let the New Year sing
    At the Old Year's grave,
Will the New Year bring
    What the Old Year gave?
Ah ! the Stranger-Year trips over the snows,
And his brow is wreathed with many a rose ;—
But how many thorns do the roses conceal
Which the roses, when withered, shall so soon reveal !

Let the New Year smile
    When the Old Year dies,
In how short a while
    Shall the smiles be sighs?
Yea ! Stranger-Year thou hast many a charm,
And thy face is fair and thy greeting warm,
But, dearer than thou—in his shroud of snows—
Is the furrowed face of the Year that goes.

Yea, bright New Year !
O'er all the earth
With song and cheer
They will hail thy birth ;
They will trust thy words in a single hour,
They will love thy face, they will laud thy power,
For the *New* has charms which the *Old* has not,
And the Stranger's face makes the Friend's forgot.

A LAUGH—AND A MOAN.

HE brook, that down the Valley
So musically drips,
Flowed never half so brightly
As the light laugh from her lips.

Her face was like the Lily,
Her heart was like the Rose,
Her eyes were like a Heaven,
Where the sunlight always glows.

She trod the earth so lightly
Her feet touched not a thorn;
Her words wore all the brightness
Of a young life's happy Morn.

A LAUGH—AND A MOAN.

Along her laughter rippled
  The melody of Joy,—
She drank from every chalice
  And tasted no alloy.

Her life was all a Laughter
  Her days were all a smile,
Her heart was pure and happy
  She knew nor gloom nor guile.

She rested on the bosom
  Of her mother, like a flower
That blooms far in a Valley
  Where no storm-clouds ever lower.

And—" Merry ! merry ! merry !"
  Rang the bells of every hour,
And—" Happy ! happy ! happy !"
  In her valley laughed the Flower.

There was not a sign of shadow,
  There was not a tear nor thorn,—
And the sweet voice of her laughter
  Filled with melody the Morn.

*   *   *   *   *   *

Years passed—'t was long—long after
  And I saw a Face at Prayer ;
There was not a sign of laughter,
  There was every sign of care.

For the Sunshine all had faded
  From the Valley and the Flower,
And the once fair face was shaded
  In life's lonely Evening hour.

And the lips that smiled with laughter
   In the Valley of the Morn,—
In the Valley of the Evening
   They were pale and sorrow-worn.

And I read the old—old lesson
   In her face and in her tears
While she sighed amid the shadows
   Of the Sunset of her years,—

All the rippling streams of laughter
   From our hearts and lips that flow
Shall be frozen, cold years after,
   Into icicles of woe.

LINES - 1875.

G O down where the wavelets are kissing the shore
   And ask of them why do they sigh ?
The poets have asked them a thousand times o'er
   But they're kissing the shore as they kissed it before,
   And they're sighing to-day and they'll sigh evermore,
Ask them what ails them ? they will not reply,
But they'll sigh on forever and never tell why !
Why does your poetry sound like a sigh ?
The waves will not answer you ; neither shall I.

Go! stand on the beach of the blue boundless deep,
When the night stars are gleaming on high,
And hear how the billows are moaning in sleep,
On the low lying strand by the surge-beaten steep,
They're moaning forever wherever they sweep ;
Ask them what ails them ? they never reply ;
They moan and so sadly, but will not tell why !
Why does your poetry sound like a sigh ?
The waves will not answer you—neither shall I ?

Go list to the breeze at the waning of day
When it passes and murmurs " Good-bye."
The dear little breeze—how it wishes to stay
Where the flowers are in bloom, where the singing birds play,
How it sighs when it flies on its wearisome way.
Ask it what ails it ? it will not reply,
Its voice is a sad one—it never told why.
Why does your poetry sound like a sigh ?
The breeze will not answer you, neither shall I.

Go watch the wild blasts as they spring from their lair,
When the shout of the storm rends the sky,
They rush o'er the earth and they ride thro' the air,
And they blight with their breath all the lovely and fair,
And they groan like the ghosts in the " land of despair."
Ask them what ails them ? they never reply,
Their voices are mournful, they will not tell why.
Why does your poetry sound like a sigh ?
The blasts will not answer you, neither shall I.

Go, stand on the rivulet's lily-fringed side,
Or list where the rivers rush by ;
The streamlets which forest trees shadow and hide,
And the rivers that roll in their oceanward tide,
Are moaning forever wherever they glide ;

Ask them what ails them ? they will not reply.
On—sad voiced, they flow, but they never tell why.
Why does your poetry sound like a sigh ?
Earth's streams will not answer you—neither shall I.

Go list to the voices of air, earth and sea,
And the voices that sound in the sky,
Their songs may be joyful to some, but to me
There's a sigh in each chord and a sigh in each key
And thousands of sighs swell their grand melody.
Ask them what ails them? they will not reply.
They sigh—sigh forever, but never tell why.
Why does your poetry sound like a sigh ?
Their lips will not answer you—neither will I.

MEMORIES.

HEY come, as the Breeze comes over the Foam
  Waking the waves that are sinking to sleep,—
  The fairest of Memories from far-away Home
    The dim dreams of faces beyond the dark deep.

They come as the stars come out in the sky
  That shimmer wherever the shadows may sweep,—
And their steps are as soft as the sound of a sigh
  And I welcome them all while I wearily weep.

They come as a song comes out of the Past
  A loved mother murmured in days that are dead—
Whose tones spirit-thrilling live on to the last
  When the Gloom of the heart wraps its Gray o'er the head,

They come like the Ghosts from the grass shrouded graves
  And they follow our footsteps on life's winding way ;—
And they murmur around us as murmur the waves
  That sigh on the shore at the dying of day.—

They come,—sad as tears to the eyes that are bright,—
  They come,—sweet as smiles to the lips that are pale,—
They come,—dim as dreams in the depths of the night,—
  They come,—fair as flowers to the Summerless vale,—

There is not a heart that is not haunted so,—
  Though far we may stray from the scenes of the Past,—
Its memories will follow wherever we go—
  And the days that were first sway the days that are Last.

"OUT OF THE DEPTHS."

LOST ! Lost ! Lost !
  The cry went up from a Sea,—
  The waves were wild with an awful wrath
  Not a light shone down on the lone ship's path ;
        The clouds hung low
        Lost ! Lost ! Lost !
  Rose wild from the hearts of the tempest-tossed.

Lost ! Lost ! Lost !
The cry floated over the waves —
Far over the pitiless waves ;
It smote on the Dark and it rended the clouds,
The billows below them were weaving white shrouds
    Out of the foam of the surge
    And the wind-voices chanted a dirge—
      Lost ! Lost ! Lost !
Wailed wilder the lips of the tempest-tossed.

      Lost ! Lost ! Lost !
Not the sign of a hope was nigh—
In the sea, in the air or the sky ;
And the lifted faces were wan and white,
There was nothing without them but Storm and Night,
    And nothing within but fear ;
    But far to a FATHER'S EAR
      Lost ! Lost ! Lost !
Floated the wail of the tempest-tossed.

      Lost ! Lost ! Lost !
Out of the depths of the sea—
Out of the Night and the Sea !
And the waves and the winds of the storm were hushed—
And the sky with the gleams of the stars was flushed,—
    Saved ! Saved ! Saved !
    And a calm and a joyous cry
    Floated up through the starry sky
In the dark—in the storm "Our Father" is nigh.

FEAST OF THE SACRED HEART.

TWO lights on a lowly Altar ;
  Two snowy cloths for a Feast ;—
Two vases of dying roses,—
  The Morning comes from the East,—
With a gleam for the folds of the Vestments
  And a grace for the face of the Priest.

The sound of a low, sweet whisper
  Floats over a little Bread,—
And trembles around a chalice,—
  And the Priest bows down his head !
O'er a Sign of White on the Altar,—
  In the cup—o'er a sign of Red.

As red as the Red of roses
  As white as the White of snows !—
But the red is the red of a surface
  Beneath which a God's blood flows ;
And the white is the white of a sunlight
  Within which a God's Flesh glows.

Ah ! Words of the olden Thursday !
  Ye come from the Far-away !—
Ye bring us the Friday's victim
  In his own love's olden way ?—
In the hand of the Priest at the altar
  His Heart finds a Home each day.

The sight of a Host uplifted !
    The silver-sound of a bell !—
The gleam of a golden chalice—
    Be glad.—sad heart ! 't is well ;
He made,—and he keeps love's promise
    With thee, all days to dwell.

From his hand to his lips that tremble,—
    From his lips to his heart a-thrill,—
Goes the little Host on its love-path
    Still doing the Father's Will ;—
And over the rim of the chalice
    The Blood flows forth,—to fill,—

The heart of the man annointed,
    With the waves of a wondrous grace ;
A silence falls on the Altar—
    An awe, on each bended face—
For the Heart that bled on Calvary
    Still beats in the Holy-Place.

The priest comes down to the railing
    Where brows are bowed in prayer,—
In the tender clasp of his fingers
    A Host lies pure and fair,—
And the hearts of Christ and the Christian
    Meet there,—and only there !

Oh ! Love ! that is deep and deathless !
    Oh ! Faith that is strong and grand !
Oh ! Hope that will shine forever,
    O'er the wastes of a weary land !—
Christ's Heart finds an earthly Heaven
    In the palm of the Priest's pure hand.

A LAND WITHOUT RUINS.

"A land without ruins is a land without memories—a land without memories is a land without history. A land that wears a laurel crown may be fair to see; but twine a few sad cypress leaves around the brow of any land, and be that land barren, beautiless and bleak, it becomes lovely in its consecrated coronet of sorrow, and it wins the sympathy of the heart and of history. Crowns of roses fade—crowns of thorns endure. Calvaries and crucifixions take deepest hold of humanity—the triumphs of might are transient—they pass and are forgotten—the sufferings of right are graven deepest on the chronicle of nations."

YES, give me the land where the ruins are spread,
And the living tread light on the hearts of the dead;
Yes, give me a land that is blest by the dust
And bright with the deeds of the down-trodden just.
Yes, give me the land where the battle's red blast
Has flashed to the future the fame of the past;
Yes, give me the land that hath legends and lays
That tell of the memories of long vanished days;
Yes, give me a land that hath story and song,
Enshrine the strife of the right with the wrong;
Yes, give me a land with a grave in each spot
And names in the graves that shall not be forgot;
Yes, give me the land of the wreck and the tomb—
There is grandeur in graves—there is glory in gloom;
For out of the gloom future brightness is born
As after the night comes the sunrise of morn;
And the graves of the dead with the grass overgrown
May yet form the footstool of liberty's throne,
And each single wreck in the war-path of might,
Shall yet be a rock in the temple of right.

IN MEMORY OF MY BROTHER.

YOUNG as the youngest who donned the Gray,
True as the truest that wore it—
Brave as the bravest he marched away,
(Hot tears on the cheeks of his mother lay),
Triumphant waved our flag one day,
He fell in the front before it.

Firm as the firmest where duty led,
He hurried without a falter ;
Bold as the boldest he fought and bled,
And the day was won—but the field was red,
And the blood of his fresh young heart was shed
On his country's hallowed altar.

On the trampled breast of the battle plain
Where the foremost ranks had wrestled,
On his pale pure face not a mark of pain,
(His mother dreams they will meet again),
The fairest form amid all the slain,
Like a child asleep—he nestled.

In the solemn shades of the wood that swept
The field where his comrades found him,
They buried him there—and the big tears crept
Into strong men's eyes that had seldom wept.
(His mother—God pity her—smiled and slept,
Dreaming her arms were around him).

A grave in the woods with the grass o'ergrown,
A grave in the heart of his mother—
His clay in the one lies lifeless and lone ;
There is not a name, there is not a stone—
And only the voice of the winds maketh moan
O'er the grave where never a flower is strewn,
But, his memory lives in the other.

A THOUGHT.

THE Summer-Rose the sun has flushed
 With crimson glory, may be sweet,—
'T is sweeter when its leaves are crushed
 Beneath the winds' and tempests' feet.

The Rose, that waves upon its tree,—
 In life, sheds perfume all around ;
More sweet the perfume floats to me
 Of roses trampled on the ground.

The waving Rose, with every breath
 Scents, carelessly the summer air,—
The wounded Rose bleeds forth in death
 A sweetness far more rich and rare.

It is a truth beyond our ken
   And yet a truth that all may read,—
It is with roses as with men
   The sweetest hearts are those that bleed.

The Flower which Bethlehem saw bloom
   Out of a Heart all full of grace
Gave never forth its full perfume
   Until the Cross became its Vase.

"GONE."

S. M. A.

GONE! and there's not a gleam of you,
Faces that float into far away,
Gone! and we can only dream of you
Each as you fade like a star away,
   Fade as a star in the sky from us,
   Vainly we look for your light again;
   Hear ye the sound of a sigh from us?
"Come" and our hearts will be bright again.

Come! and gaze on our face once more,
Bring us the smiles of the olden days;—
Come! and shine in your place once more,
And, change the dark into golden days—
   Gone! Gone! Gone! Joy is fled for us,
   Gone into the night of the nevermore,
   And darkness rests where you shed for us
A light we will miss *for ever more.*

Faces ! ye come in the night to us,
Shadows ! ye float in the sky of sleep,
Shadows ! ye bring nothing bright to us,
Faces ! ye are but the sigh of sleep.

    Gone ! and there 's not a gleam of you,
    Faces that float into the far away ;
    Gone ! and we only can dream of you
    Till we sink like you and the stars away.

FEAST OF THE ASSUMPTION.

" A NIGHT-PRAYER."

ARK ! Dark ! Dark !
The sun is set ; the Day is dead,
    Thy Feast has fled ;
My eyes are wet, with tears unshed
    I bow my head ;
Where the star-fringed shadows softly sway,
    I bend my knee,
And, like a homesick child, I pray,
    Mary ! to Thee.

    Dark ! Dark ! Dark !
And, all the Day,—since white-robed Priest
    In farthest East,
In dawn's first ray,—began the Feast,—
    I—I the least,—
Thy least, and last and lowest child
    I called on Thee !
Virgin ! did'st hear ? my words were wild ;
    Did'st think of me ?

Dark ! Dark ! Dark !
Alas ! and no !—the Angels bright
    With wings as white
As a dream of snow—in Love and Light
    Flashed on thy sight ;
They shone, like stars around Thee ! Queen !—
    I knelt afar—
A Shadow only dims the scene
    Where shines a star !

Dark ! Dark ! Dark !
And all day long,—beyond the sky
    Sweet,—pure,—and high
The Angels' song swept sounding by
    Triumphantly ;—
And when such music filled thy ear
    Rose round thy throne,—
How could I hope that thou would'st hear
    My far, faint moan?

Dark ! Dark ! Dark !
And all day long,—where altars stand
    Or poor or grand
A countless throng—from every land
    With lifted hand,
Winged hymns to Thee from sorrow's vale
    In glad acclaim,—
How could'st thou hear my lone lips wail
    Thy sweet, pure Name?

Dark ! Dark ! Dark !
Alas ! and no,—Thou did'st not hear
    Nor bend thy ear,—
To prayer of woe—as mine so drear;
    For hearts more dear

Hid me from hearing and from sight
    This bright Feast-day ;—
Wilt hear me, Mother if in its Night
    I kneel and pray ?

    Dark ! Dark ! Dark !
The sun is set,—the Day is dead
    Thy feast hath fled ;
My eyes are wet with the tears I shed—
    I bow my head ;—
Angels and Altars hailed Thee Queen
    All day ;—ah ! be
To-night what thou hast ever been
    A Mother to me !

    Dark ! Dark ! Dark !
Thy Queenly Crown,—in angel's sight
    Is fair and bright ;
Ah ! lay it down ; for oh ! to-night
    Its jewelled light
Shines not as the tender love-light shines
    O Mary ! mild,
In the mother's eyes, whose pure heart pines
    For poor, lost child !

    Dark ! Dark ! Dark !
Sceptre in hand,—Thou dost hold sway
    Fore'er and aye.
In angel-land,—but fair Queen ! pray !
    Lay it away,—
Let thy sceptre wave in the realms above
    Where angels are ;
But, Mother ! fold in thine arms of love
    Thy child afar !

Dark ! Dark ! Dark !
Mary ! I call ! Wilt hear the Prayer
 My poor lips dare !
Yea ! be to all,—a Queen most fair,
 Crown, sceptre bear !
But look on me with a Mother's eyes
 From Heaven's bliss ;—
And waft to me from the starry skies
 A mother's kiss !

Dark ! Dark ! Dark !
The Sun's is set—the Day is dead ;
 Her feast has fled ;—
Can she forget the sweet blood shed,
 The last words said
That evening—"Woman ! behold thy Son" !
 Oh ! priceless Right !
Of all His children, the last, least one
 Is heard to-night.

SURSUM · CORDA.

EARY hearts ! weary hearts ! by the cares of life
 oppressed,
Ye are wand'ring in the shadows—ye are sighing for
 a rest :
There is darkness in the heavens, and the earth is bleak
below,
And the joys we taste to-day may to-morrow turn to woe.
 Weary Hearts ! God is Rest.

Lonely Hearts ! lonely hearts ! this is but a land of grief ;
Ye are pining for repose—ye are longing for relief :
What the world hath never given—Kneel, and ask of God
above,
And your grief shall turn to gladness—if you lean upon
His love.
Lonely Hearts ! God is Love.

Restless Hearts ! restless hearts ! ye are toiling night and day,
And the flowers of life all withered, leave but thorns along
your way :
Ye are waiting—ye are wailing till your toilings all shall
cease,
And your ev'ry restless beating is a sad—sad prayer for peace.
'Restless Heart ! God is Peace.

Breaking Hearts ! broken hearts ! ye are desolate and lone,
And low voices from the Past o'er your present ruins moan !
In the sweetest of your pleasures there was bitterest alloy—
And a starless night hath followed on the sunset of your joy.
Broken Hearts ! God is Joy.

Homeless Hearts ! homeless hearts ! through the dreary,
dreary years,
Ye are lonely, lonely wand'rers, and your way is wet with
tears ;
In bright or blighted places, wheresoever ye may roam,
Ye look away from earth-land and ye murmur "where is
home ?"
Homeless Hearts ! God is Home.

"PRESENTIMENT."   .

"MY SISTER."·

OMETH a Voice from a Far-land !
Beautiful, sad and low,
Shineth a Light from the star-land !
Down on the Night of my love,
And a white Hand, with a garland
Biddeth my spirit to go.

Away and afar from the Night-land
Where sorrow o'ershadows my way,
To the splendors and skies of the Light-land
Where reigneth Eternity's Day,
To the cloudless and shadowless Bright-land
Whose sun never passeth away.   .

And *I* knew the voice ;—not a sweeter
On earth or in heaven can be ;
And never did shadow pass fleeter
Than it,—and its strange melody ;
And I know I must hasten to meet her,
"Yea ! *Sister!* Thou callest to me " !

And *I* saw the Light ;—'t was not seeming,
It flashed from the crown that she wore,
And the brow, that, with jewels, was gleaming
My lips had kissed often of yore ;
And the eyes, that with rapture were beaming,
Had smiled on me sweetly before.

And I saw the Hand with the Garland,
　　Ethel's Hand—holy and fair ;
Who went long ago to the Far-land
　　To weave me the wreath I shall wear ;—
And, to-night, I look up to the Star-land
　　And pray that I soon may be there.

————————

A CHILD'S WISH.

BEFORE AN ALTAR.

WISH I was the little key,
　　That locks Love's Captive in,
Ar d lets him out to go and free
　　A sinful heart from sin.—

I wish I were the little bell,
　　That tinkles for the Host,—
When GOD comes down each day to dwell
　　With hearts He loves the most.—

I wish I were the chalice fair,
　　That holds the Blood of Love,
When every flash lights holy prayer
　　Upon its way above.—

I wish I were the little flower
　　So near the Host's sweet Face—
Or like the light that half an hour
　　Burns on the shrine of grace.—

I wish I was the Altar, where
    As on His mother's breast,
Christ nestles, like a child, fore'er
    In Eucharistic rest.

But, Oh ! my GOD I wish the most
    That my poor heart may be,
A home all holy for each Host
    That comes in love to me.

I OFTEN WONDER WHY 'TIS SO.

SOME find work where some find rest
    And so the weary world goes on ;—
I sometimes wonder which is best?
    The answer comes when life is gone.

Some eyes sleep when some eyes wake,
    And so the dreary night-hours go ;
Some hearts beat where some hearts break—
    I often wonder why 't is so.

Some wills faint where some wills fight,—
    Some love the tent,—and some, the field :—
I often wonder who are right,—
    The ones who strive,—or those, who yield?

Some hands fold where other hands
    Are lifted bravely in the strife ;—
And so thro' ages and thro' lands
    Move on the two extremes of life.

Some feet halt where some feet tread,
  In tireless march, a thorny way ;—
Some struggle on where some have fled ;—
  Some seek,—when others shun the fray.

Some swords rust where others clash,—
  Some fall back where some move on,—
Some flags furl where others flash
  Until the battle has been won.

Some sleep on while others keep
  The vigils of the true and brave :—
They will not rest till roses creep
  Around their name above a grave.

WAKE ME A SONG.

OUT of the Silences wake me a song,
  Beautiful, sad, and soft and low ;
Let the loveliest music sound along,
  And wing each note with a wail of woe.
          Dim and drear
          As hope's last tear,
Out of the Silences wake me a hymn,
Whose sounds are like shadows soft and dim.

Out of the Stillnesses in your heart—
A thousand songs are sleeping there,—
Wake me a song, thou child of art !
The song of a hope in a last despair,
Dark and low,
A chant of woe,
Out of the stillness, tone by tone,
Cold as a snow-flake, low as a moan.

Out of the darkness, flash me a song,
Brightly dark and darkly bright ;—
Let it sweep as a lone star sweeps along
The mystical shadows of the night.
Sing it sweet,
Where nothing is drear, or dark or dim,
And earth-song soars into heavenly hymn.

"IN MEMORIAM."

O ! Heart of mine ! the way is long,—
The night is dark,—the place is far ;
Go ! kneel and pray, or chant a song
Beside two graves where Mary's star
Shines o'er two children's hearts at rest
With Mary's medals on their breast.

Go ! Heart ! those children loved you so,
  Their little lips prayed oft for you !
But ah ! those necks are lying low
  Round which you twined the badge of Blue.
Go to their graves,—this Virgin's feast
  With poet's song and prayer of Priest.

Go ! like a pilgrim to a shrine
  For that is holy ground where sleep
Children of Mary and of thine.
    Go ! kneel, and pray and sing and weep ;—
Last summer how their faces smiled
  When each was blessed as Mary's child.
      *   *   *   *   *
My heart hath gone ! I cannot sing !
  Beside those children's grave, song dies ;
Hush ! Poet !   Priest ! Prayer hath a wing
  To pass the stars and reach the skies ;—
Sweet children ! from the land of light
  Look down and bless my Heart to-night.

REVERIE.

E laugh when our souls are the saddest,
  We shroud all our griefs in a smile ;
Our voices may warble their gladdest,
  And our souls mourn in anguish the while.

And our eyes wear a summer's bright glory,
　　When winter is wailing beneath ; ˙
And we tell not the world the sad story
　　Of the thorn hidden back of the wreath.

Ah ! fast flow the moments of laughter,
　　And bright as the brook to the sea ;
But ah ! the dark hours that come after
　　Of moaning for you and for me.

Yea, swift as the sunshine, and fleeting
　　As birds, fly the moments of glee !
And we smile ; — and mayhaps grief is sleeting
　　Its ice upon you and on me.

And the clouds of the tempest are shifting
　　O'er the heart, tho' the face may be bright ;
And the snows of woe's winter are drifting
　　Our souls ; and each day hides a night.

For ah ! when our souls are enjoying
　　The mirth which our faces reveal,
There is something—a something – alloying
　　The sweetness of joy that we feel.

Life's loveliest sky hides the thunder,
　　Whose bolt in a moment may fall,
And our path may be flowery ; but under
　　The flowers there are thorns for us all.

Ah ! 'tis hard when our beautiful dreamings,
　　That flash down the valley of Night,
Wave their wing when the gloom hides their gleaming,
　　And leave us, like eagles in flight ;

And fly far away unreturning,
    And leave us in terror and tears,
While vain is the spirit's wild yearning
    That they may come back in the years.

Come back! did I say it? but never
    Do eagles come back to the cage:
They have gone—they have gone—and forever!
    Does youth come back ever to age?

No! a joy that has left us in sorrow
    Smiles never again on our way;
But we meet in the farthest To-morrow
    The face of the grief of To-day.

The brightness whose tremulous glimmer
    Has faded—we cannot recall;
And the Light that grows dimmer and dimmer—
    When gone—'tis forever and all.

Not a ray of it anywhere lingers,
    Not a gleam of it gilds the vast gloom,
Youth's roses perfume not the fingers
    . Of age groping nigh to the tomb.

For "the memory of joy is a sadness"—
    The dim twilight after the day;—
And the grave where we bury a gladness
    Sends a grief, like a ghost, on our way.

No day shall return that has faded,
    The dead come not back from the tomb;
The vale of each life must be shaded,
    That we may see best from the gloom.

The height of the home of our glory
    All radiant with splendors of light—
That we may read clearly life's story—
    "The Dark is the Dawn of the Bright."

TEARS

HE tears that trickled down our eyes,
  They do not touch the earth to-day;
But soar like angels to the skies,—
  And like the angels, may not die ;
    For ah ! our immortality
    Flows thro' each tear,—sounds in each sigh.

What waves of tears surge o'er the deep
  Of sorrow, in our restless souls !
And they are strong, not weak, who weep,
  Those drops from out the sea that rolls
    Within their hearts forevermore ;
    Without a depth—without a shore.

But ah ! the tears that are not wept,
  The tears that never outward fall ;
The tears that grief for years has kept
  Within us—they are best of all :
    The tears our eyes shall never know,
    Are dearer than the tears that flow.

Each night upon earth's flowers below,
  The dew comes down from darkest skies,
And every night our tears of woe
  Go up like dews to Paradise,
    To keep in bloom, and make more fair,
    The flowers of crowns we yet shall wear.

For ah ! the surest way to God
  Is up the lonely streams of tears,
That flow, when bending 'neath His rod,
  And fill the tide of earthly years.
        On laughter's billows hearts are tossed,
        On waves of tears no heart is lost.

Flow on, ye tears ! and bear me home ;
  Flow not ! ye tears of deeper woe ;
Flow on, ye tears ! that are but foam
  Of deeper waves that will not flow.
        A little while—I reach the shore
        Where tears flow not forevermore !

LINES.

TWO LOVES.

WO Loves came up a long, wide aisle
  And knelt at a low, white gate ;
One—tender and true, with the shyest smile,
  One—strong, true and elate.

        Two lips spoke in a firm, true way
          And two lips answered soft and low,
        In one true hand such a little hand lay
          Fluttering, frail as a flake of snow.

One stately head bent humbly there,
　Stilled were the throbbings of human love ,
One head drooped down like a lily fair,
　Two prayers went, wing to wing, above.

　　God blest them both in the holy place,
　　　A long—brief moment ;—the rite was done;
　　On the human love fell the heavenly grace,
　　　Making two hearts forever one.

Between two lengthening rows of smiles,
　One sweetly shy, one proud, elate,—
Two Loves passed down the long, wide aisles,—
　Will they ever forget the low, white gate ?

THE LAND WE LOVE.

LAND of the gentle and brave !
　Our love is as wide as thy woe ;
It deepens beside every grave
　Where the heart of a hero lies low.

　Land of the sunniest skies !
　　Our love glows the more for thy gloom ;
　Our hearts by the saddest of ties,
　　Cling closest to thee in thy doom.

Land where the desolate weep
  In a sorrow no voice may console,
Our tears are but streams making deep
  The ocean of love in our soul.

Land where the victor's flag waves,
  Where only the dead are the free ;
Each link of the chain that enslaves,
  But binds us to them and to thee.

Land where the Sign of the Cross
  Its shadow hath everywhere shed,
We measure our love by thy loss,—
  Thy loss—by the graves of our dead

A BLESSING.

E you near, or be you far !
Let my Blessing,—like a Star,
  Shine upon you everywhere !
And in each lone Evening-hour
When the twilight folds the flower,
  I will fold thy name in Prayer.

In the Dark and in the Day—
To my heart you know the way,
  Sorrow's pale hand keeps the key;--
In your sorrow or your sin
You may always enter in,—
  I will keep a place for thee.

If God's blessing pass away
From your spirit ;—if you stray
   From his presence,—do not wait.
Come to my heart,—for I keep,
For the hearts that wail and weep,
   Ever opened wide, a Gate.

In your joys,—to others go,—
When your feet walk ways of woe
   Only then come back to me ;—
I will give you tear for tear
And our tears shall more endear
   Thee to me and me to thee.

For I make my heart the Home
Of all hearts in grief that come
   Seeking refuge and a Rest.
Do not fear me,—for you know,—
Be your footsteps e'er so low
   I know yours, of all, the best.

Once you came ;—and you brought sin ;—
Did not my hand lead you in—
   Into God's Heart, thro' my own ?
Did not my voice speak a word
You, for years, had never heard,—
   Mystic word in Mercy's tone ?

And a grace fell on your brow
And I heard your murmured vow,—
   When I whispered : "Go in peace,"
"Go in peace,—and sin no more"—
   Did you not touch mercy's shore ?
   Did not sin's wild tempest cease ?

Go then!—thou art good and pure,—•
If thou e'er shouldst fall—be sure—
   Back to me thy footsteps trace!
In my heart for year and year
Be thou far away or near
   I shall keep for thee—a place.

Yes! I bless you—near or far—
And my blessing,—like a star
   Shall shine on you everywhere,—
And in many a holy hour,—
As the sunshine folds the flower,
   I will fold thy Heart in Prayer.

ERIN'S FLAG.

UNROLL Erin's flag! fling its folds to the breeze!
  Let it float o'er the land, let it flash o'er the seas;
  Lift it out of the dust—let it wave as of yore,
   When its chiefs with their clans stood around it and
      swore
That never!—no!—never, while God gave them life,
And they had an arm and a sword for the strife,
That never!—no!—never, that Banner should yield
As long as the heart of a Celt was its shield;
While the hand of a Celt had a weapon to wield,
And his last drop of blood was unshed on the field.

Lift it up! wave it high!—'tis as bright as of old!
Not a stain on its Green, not a blot on its gold,
Tho' the woes and the wrongs of three hundred long years
Have drenched Erin's Sunburst with blood and with tears!
Though the clouds of oppression enshroud it in gloom,
And around it the thunders of Tyranny boom.
Look aloft! look aloft! lo! the clouds drifting by,
There's a gleam through the gloom, there's a light in the sky.
'Tis the Sunburst resplendent—far, flashing on high!
Erin's dark night is waning; her day dawn is nigh!

Lift it up! lift it up! the old Banner of Green!
The blood of its sons has but brightened its sheen;
What!—though the Tyrant has trampled it down,
Are its folds not emblazoned with deeds of renown?
What!—though for ages it droops in the dust,
Shall it droop thus forever?—no! no! God is just!
Take it up! take it up! from the tyrant's foul tread,
Let him tear the Green Flag—we will snatch its last shred,
And beneath it we'll bleed as our forefathers bled,
And we'll vow by the dust in the graves of our dead.

And we'll swear by the blood which the Briton has shed—
And we'll vow by the wrecks which through Erin he spread—
And we'll swear by the thousands who, famished, unfed,
Died down in the ditches—wild-howling for bread.
And we'll vow by our heroes, whose spirits have fled;
And we'll swear by the bones in each coffinless bed,
That we'll battle the Briton through danger and dread;
That we'll cling to the cause which we glory to wed,
'Till the gleam of our steel and the shock of our lead
Shall prove to our foe that we meant what we said—
That we'll lift up the Green, and we'll tear down the Red.

Lift up the Green Flag! oh! it wants to go nome;
Full long has its lot been to wander and roam;
It has followed the fate of its sons o'er the world,
But its folds, like their hopes, are not faded nor furled;
Like a weary-winged bird, to the East and the West,
It has flitted and fled—but it never shall rest,
'Till, pluming its pinions, it sweeps o'er the main,
And speeds to the shores of its old home again,
Where its fetterless folds, o'er each mountain and plain,
Shall wave with a glory that never shall wane.

Take it up! take it up! bear it back from afar—
That Banner must blaze 'mid the lightnings of war;
Lay your hands on its folds, lift your gaze to the sky,
And swear that you'll bear it triumphant or die,
And shout to the clans scattered far o'er the earth,
To join in the march to the land of their birth;
And wherever the Exiles, 'neath heaven's broad dome,
Have been fated to suffer, to sorrow and roam,
They'll bound on the sea, and away o'er the foam,
They'll sail to the music of "Home, sweet Home"!

JULY 9TH, 1872.

ETWEEN two pillared clouds of Gold
  The Beautiful Gates of Evening swung,—
And far and wide, from flashing fold
  The half-furled Banners of Light, that hung,—
O'er green of wood and gray of wold—
And over the Blue where the river rolled
  The fading gleams of their Glory, flung.

The sky wore not a frown all day
  To mar the smile of the Morning-tide,
The soft-voiced winds sang joyous lay
  You never would think they had ever sighed ;—
The stream went on its sunlit way
In ripples of laughter ; happy they
  As the hearts that met at Riverside.

No cloudlet in the sky serene !
  Not a silver speck in the golden hue !
But where the woods waved low and green,
  And seldom would let the sunlight through,
Sweet shadows fell, and in their screen
The faces of children might be seen
  And the flash of ribbons of blue.

It was a children's simple feast,—
    Yet many were there whose faces told
How far they are from Childhood's East
    Who have reached the Evening of the Old!
And Father,—Mother,—Sister,—Priest,—
They seemed all day like the very least
    Of the little children of the fold.—

The old forgot they were not young
    The young forgot they would e'er be old,
And all day long the trees among
    Where'er their footsteps stayed or strolled
Came wittiest word from tireless tongue
And the merriest peals of laughter rung
    Where the woods drooped low and the river rolled.

No cloud upon the faces there,—
    Not a sorrow came from its hiding place
To cast the shadow of a care
    On the fair sweet brows in that fairest place ;
For in the sky and in the air
And in their spirits and everywhere
    Joy reigned in the fullness of her grace.

The Day was long,—but ah! too brief!
    Swift to the West bright-winged she fled,—
Too soon on ev'ry look and leaf
    The last rays flushed which her plumage shed
From an Evening cloud,—was it a sign of grief?
And the bright Day passed,—is there much relief
    That its Dream dies not when its gleam is dead?—

Great sky! thou art a Prophet still!
    And by thy shadows and by thy rays
We read the future if we will

And all the fates of our future ways,—
To-morrows meet us in vale and hill,—
And under the trees and by the rill
   Thou givest the sign of our coming days.

That Evening-cloud was a Sign I ween,—
   For the sister of that Summer-Day
Shall come next year to the self-same scene—
   The winds will sing the self-same lay—
The self-same woods will wave as green,—
And Riverside! thy skies serene
Shall robe thee again in a golden sheen
Yet though thy shadows may weave a screen
Where the children's faces may be seen
Thou ne'er shall be as thou hast been
   For a Face they loved has passed away.

A DEATH.

CRUSHED with a burden of woe,
   Wrecked in the tempest of sin.
Death came, and two lips murmured low,
"Ah! once I was white as the snow,
In the happy and pure long-ago;
But they say God is sweet—is it so?
   Will he let a poor wayward one in"?

" In where the innocent are,
 Ah ! Justice stands guard at the gate—
 Does it mock at a poor sinner's fate—
Alas ! I have fallen so far !
 Oh God ! Oh my God ! 'Tis too late !
I have fallen as falls a lost star,
The sky does not miss the gone gleam ;
But my heart, like the lost star, can dream
Of the sky it has fall'n from.   Nay !
I have wandered too far—far away,
Oh ! would that my mother were here ;
Is God like a mother ? Has he
Any love for a sinner like me "?

Her face wore the wildness of woe—
 Her words, the wild tones of despair;
Ah ! how can a heart sink so low,
 How a face that was once bright and so fair,
 Can be furrowed and darkened with care?
Wild rushed the hot tears from her eyes,
From her lips rushed the wildest of sighs,
Her poor heart was broken ; but then
Her God was far gentler than men.

A voice whispered low at her side,
 "Child ! God is more gentle than men,
He watches by Passion's dark tide,
 He sees a wreck drifting—and then
He beckons with hand and with voice,
 And He sees the poor wreck floating in
To the haven on Mercy's bright shore,
And he whispers the whisper of yore :
'The angels of Heaven rejoice
 O'er the sinner repenting of sin.' "

* * * *

And a silence eame down for awhile,
  And her lips they were moving in prayer,
And her face it wore just such a smile,
  As, perhaps, it was oft wont to wear,
Ere the heart of the girl knew a guile,
Ere the soul of the girl knew the wile,
  That had led her to Passion's despair.

Death's shadows crept over her face,
  And softened the hard marks of care ;
Repentance had won a last grace,
  And the Angel of Mercy stood there.

IN MEMORIAM.

DAVID J. RYAN, C. S. A.

THOU art sleeping, Brother, sleeping
    In thy lonely battle grave ;
Shadows o'er the past are creeping,
Death, the reaper, still is reaping,
Years have swept, and years are sweeping
Many a memory from my keeping,
But I'm waiting still, and weeping
    For my Beautiful and Brave.

When the battle songs were chaunted,
  And war's stirring tocsin pealed,
By those songs thy heart was haunted,
And thy spirit, proud, undaunted,
Clamored wildly—wildly panted ;
" Mother ! let my wish be granted ;
I will ne'er be mocked and taunted
That I feared to meet our vaunted
  Foemen on the bloody field."

" They are thronging, mother ! thronging,
  To a thousand fields of fame ;
Let me go—'tis wrong and wronging
God and thee to crush this longing ;
On the muster-roll of glory,
In my country's future story,
On the field of battle gory
  I must consecrate my name.

" Mother ! gird my sword around me,
  Kiss thy soldier-boy ' good-bye.' "
In her arms she wildly wound thee—
To thy birth-land's cause she bound thee—
With fond prayers and blessings crowned thee
And she sobbed : " When foes surround thee,
If you fall, I'll know they found thee,
  Where the bravest love to die."

At the altar of their nation,
  Stood that mother and her son ;
He, the victim of oblation ;
Panting for his immolation ;
She, in priestess' holy station,

Weeping words of consecration,
While God smiled his approbation,
Blessed the boy's self-abnegation,
Cheered the mother's desolation,
    When the sacrifice was done.

Forth, like many a noble other,
    Went he, whispering soft and low
"Good-bye—pray for me, my mother ;
Sister ! kiss me—farewell, brother " ;
And he strove his grief to smother.
Forth, with footsteps firm and fearless,
And his parting gaze was tearless,
Though his heart was lone and cheerless,
    Thus from all he loved to go.

Lo ! yon flag of freedom flashing
    In the sunny Southern sky :
On—to death and glory dashing,
On—where swords are clanging, clashing.
On—where balls are crushing, crashing,
On—'mid perils dread, appalling,
On—they 're falling, falling, falling,
On—they 're growing fewer, fewer,
On—their hearts beat all the truer,
    On—on—on, —no fear, no falter,
    On—though round the battle-altar,
There were wounded victims moaning,
There were dying soldiers groaning ;—
On,—right on,—death's danger braving,
Warring where their flag was waving,
While Baptismal-blood was laving
    All that field of death and slaughter ;—
On—still on ;—that bloody laver

Made them braver and made them braver,-
On—with never a halt or waver,—
On in battle—bleeding—bounding
While the glorious shout swept sounding
    " We will win the day or die."

And they won it ;—routed,—riven
    Reeled the foemen's proud array :
They had struggled hard,—and striven,
Blood in torrents they had given,
But their ranks dispersed and driven
    Fled, in sullenness, away.

Many a heart was lonely lying
    That would never throb again,—
Some were dead,—and some were dying
Those were silent,—these were sighing
Thus to die alone,—unattended,
.Unbewept and unbefriended
    On that bloody battle-plain.

When the twilight sadly, slowly
    Wrapped its mantle o'er them all,
Thousands,—thousands lying lowly
Hushed in silence deep and holy,—
There was one,—his blood was flowing
And his last of life was going,—
And his pulse faint,—fainter beating
Told his hours were few and fleeting,—
And his brow grew white and whiter
While his eyes grew strangely brighter,—
There he lay—like infant dreaming
With his sword beside him gleaming,—
For the hand, in life, that grasped it

True, in death, still fondly clasped it ;—
There his comrades found him lying
'Mid the heaps of dead and dying,
And the sternest bent down weeping
O'er the lonely sleeper sleeping :
'Twas the midnight ;—stars shone round him,—
And they told us how they found him
      Where the bravest love to fall.

Where the woods, like banners bending,
      Drooped in starlight and in gloom,—
There, when that sad night was ending
And the faint, far dawn was blending
With the stars now fast descending,—
There,—they mute and mournful bore him
With the stars and shadows o'er him,—
And they laid him down—so tender—
And the next day's sun, in splendor
      Flashed above my brother's tomb.

WHAT?

TO ETHEL.

T the golden gates of the Visions
      I knelt me adown, one day,
But sudden my prayer was a silence,
      For I heard from the " Far away,"
The murmur of many voices
      And a silvery censer's sway.

I bowed in awe, and I listened—
   The deeps of my soul were stirred,
But deepest of all was the meaning
   Of the far off music I heard,
And yet it was stiller than silence,—
   Its notes were the "Dream of a Word."

A word that is whispered in Heaven
   But cannot be heard below,
It lives on the lips of the angels
   Where'er their pure wings glow,
Yet only the "Dream of its Echo"
   Ever reaches this valley of woe.

But I know the Word and its meaning,—
   I reached to its height that day,
When prayer sank into a silence
   And my heart was so far away,
But I may not murmur the music,
   Nor the Word may my lips yet say.

But some day far in the future,
   And up from the dust of the dead,
And out of my lips when speechless
   The mystical word shall be said,
'Twill come to thee, still as a spirit,
   When the soul of the Bard has fled.

A "THOUGHT-FLOWER."

ILENTLY,—shadowly, some lives go,—
And the sound of their voices is all unheard,—
Or if heard at all, 'tis as faint as the flow
Of beautiful waves which no storm hath stirred.
Deep lives these,—
As the pearl-strewn seas.

Softly and noiselessly some feet tread
Lone ways on earth, without leaving a mark,—
They move 'mid the living,—they pass to the dead
As still as the gleam of a star thro' the dark.
Sweet lives those
In their strange repose.

Calmly and lowly some hearts beat,
And none may know that they beat at all ;—
They muffle their music whenever they meet
A few in a hut or a crowd in a hall.
Great hearts those—
God only knows !

Soundlessly,—shadowly, such move on,
Dim as the dream of a child asleep ;
And no one knoweth 'till they are gone
How lofty their souls,—their hearts how deep ;—
Bright souls these—
God only sees.

Lonely and hiddenly in the world,—
 Tho' in the world 'tis their lot to stay,—
The tremulous wings of their hearts are furled
 Until they fly from the world away
   And find their rest
    On "Our Father's" breast,—
Where earth's unknown shall be known the best,
And the hidden hearts shall be brightest blest.

———————

THE MASTER'S VOICE.

THE waves were weary, and they went to sleep;
  The winds were hushed,
  The starlight flushed
The furrowed face of all the mighty deep,

The billows yester eve so dark and wild,
  Wore strangely now—
  A calm upon their brow,
Like that which rests upon a cradled child.

The sky was bright, and every single star,
  With gleaming face,
  Was in its place,
And looked upon the sea—so fair and far.

And all was still—still as a temple dim—
  When low and faint
  As murmurs plaint
Dies the last note of the vesper hymn.

A bark slept on the sea,—and in the bark
  Slept Mary's Son—
   The only One
Whose Face is light! where all, all else, is dark.

His brow was heavenward turned, His face was fair;
  He dreamed of me
   On that still sea—
The stars He made were gleaming through His hair.

And, lo! a moan moved o'er the mighty deep,
  The sky grew dark!
   The little bark
Felt all the waves awaking from their sleep.

The winds wailed wild, and wilder billows beat;
  The bark was tossed:
   Shall all be lost?
But Mary's Son slept on, serene and sweet.

The tempest raged in all its mighty wrath,
  The winds howled on,
   All hope seemed gone,
And darker waves surged round the bark's lone patn,

The sleeper woke! He gazed upon the deep—
  He whispered: "Peace!
   Winds—wild waves, cease!
Be still"! The tempest fled—the ocean fell asleep.

And, ah! when human hearts by storms are tossed;
  When life's lone bark
   Drifts through the dark,
And 'mid the wildest·waves where all seems lost,

He now, as then, with words of power and peace,
    Murmurs: "Stormy deep,
    Be still—still—and sleep"!
And, lo! a great calm comes—the tempest's perils cease.

DEATH.

OUT of the shadows of sadness,
  to the sunshine of gladness,
   Into the light of the blest;
Out of a land very dreary,
Out of the world very weary,
  Into the Rapture of Rest.

    Out of To-day's sin and sorrow,
    Into a blissful To-morrow,
      Into a day without gloom ;—
    Out of a land filled with sighing,
    Land of the dead and the dying,
      Into a land without tomb.

Out of a life of commotion
Tempest-swept oft as the ocean,
  Dark with the wrecks drifting o'er,
Into a land calm and quiet,
Never a storm cometh night it,
  Never a wreck on its shore.

Out of a land in whose bowers
Perish and fade all the flowers,
　　Out of the land of decay—
·　Into the Eden where fairest
Of flowerlets—and sweetest and rarest
　　Never shall wither away.

Out of the world of the wailing
Thronged with the anguished and ailing,
　Out of the world of the sad,
Into the world that rejoices,
World of bright visions and voices,
　Into the world of the glad.

Out of a life ever mournful,
Out of a land very lornful
　　Where in bleak exile we roam ;—
Into a joy-land above us
Where there's a Father to love us,—
　　Into our Home,—"Sweet Home."

THE ROSARY OF MY TEARS.

SOME reckon their age by years,
　Some measure their life by art ;
But some tell their days by the flow of their tears,
　And their lives by the moans of their heart.

The dials of earth may show
The length,—not the depth of years,
Few or many they come,—few or many they go,
But Time is best measured by tears.

Ah ! not by the silver gray
That creeps thro' the sunny hair,
And not by the scenes that we pass on our way
And not by the furrows, the fingers of care

On forehead and face have made.
Not so do we count our years ;
Not by the sun of the earth, but the shade
Of our souls, and the fall of our tears.

For the young are oft-times old,
Though their brows be bright and fair ;
While their blood beats warm, their hearts are cold—
O'er them the Spring—but Winter is there.

And the old are oft-times young,
When their hair is thin and white ;
And they sing in age, as in youth they sung,
And they laugh, for their cross was light.

But, bead by bead, I tell
The Rosary of my years ;
From a cross—to a cross they lead ; 'tis well,
And they're blest with a blessing of tears.

Better a day of strife,
Than a century of sleep ;
Give me instead of a long stream of life
The tempests and tears of the deep.

A thousand joys may foam
On the billows of all the years ;
But never the foam brings the lone back home,—
It reaches the haven through tears.

A REVERIE.

THOSE hearts of ours—how strange ! how strange !
How they yearn to ramble and love to range
Down through the vales of the years long gone,
Up through the future that fast rolls on.

To-days are dull—so they wend their ways
Back to their beautiful yesterdays ;
The present is blank—so they wing their flight
To future to-morrows where all seems bright.

Build them a bright and beautiful home,
They'll soon grow weary and want to roam ;
Find them a spot without sorrow or pain,
They may stay a day, but they're off again.

Those hearts of ours—how wild ! how wild !
They're as hard to tame as an Indian child ;
They're as restless as waves on the sounding sea,
Like the breeze and the bird—are they fickle and free.

Those hearts of ours—how lone ! how lone !
Ever, forever they mourn and moan ;
Let them revel in joy—let them riot in cheer,
The revelry o'er they're all the more drear.

Those hearts of ours—how warm ! how warm !
Like the sun's bright rays, like the summer's charm ;
How they beam and burn ! how they gleam and glow !
Their flash and flame hide but ashes below.

Those hearts of ours—how cold ! how cold !
Like December's snow on the waste or wold ;
And though our Decembers melt soon into May—
Hearts know Decembers that pass not away.

Those hearts of ours—how deep ! how deep !
You may sound the sea where the corals sleep,
Where never a billow hath rumbled or rolled—
Depths still the deeper our hearts hide and hold.

Where the wild storm's tramp hath ne'er been known
The wrecks of the sea lie low and lone ;
Thus the heart's surface may sparkle and glow,
There are wrecks far down,—there are graves below.

Those hearts of ours—but, after all,
How shallow and narrow, how tiny and small ;
Like scantiest streamlet or Summer's least rill
They're as easy to empty,—as easy to fill.

One hour of storm and how the streams pour !
One hour of sun and the streams are no more ;
One little grief ;—how the tears gush and glide !
One smile, flow they ever so fast ;—they are dried.

Those hearts of ours—how wise ! how wise !
They can lift their thoughts 'till they touch the skies ;
They can sink their shafts, like a miner bold,
Where wisdom's mines hide their pearls and gold.

Aloft they soar with undazzled gaze
Where the halls of the Day-King burn and blaze ;
Or they fly with a wing that will never fail
O'er the sky's dark sea where the star-ships sail.

Those hearts of ours—what fools ! what fools !
How they laugh at wisdom, her cant and rules !
How they waste their powers, and when wasted grieve
For what they have squandered but cannot retrieve.

Those hearts of ours—how strong ! how strong !
Let a thousand sorrows around them throng,
They can bear them all, and a thousand more,
And they're stronger then than they were before.

Those hearts of ours—how weak ! how weak !
But a single word of unkindness speak,
Like a poisoned shaft,—like a viper's fang
That one slight word leaves a life-long pang.

Those hearts of ours—but I've said enough,
As I find that my rhyme grows rude and rough ;
I'll rest me now, but I'll come again
Some other day to resume my strain.

———————————

OLD TREES.

LD trees ! old trees ! in your mystic gloom
  There's many a warrior laid,
And many a nameless and lonely tomb
  Is sheltered beneath your shade.
Old trees ! old trees ! without pomp or prayer
  We buried the brave and the true
We fired a volley and left them there
  To rest, old trees, with you.

Old trees, old trees, keep watch and ward
  Over each grass grown bed,
'Tis a glory, old trees, to stand as guard
  Over our Southern Dead ;
Old trees, old trees, we shall pass away
  Like the leaves you yearly shed,
But ye ! lone sentinels, still must stay,
  Old trees ! to guard " Our Dead."

A THOUGHT.

HERE never was a Valley without a faded flower,
  There never was a Heaven without some little
    cloud,
The face of day may flash with light in any morning
    hour,
  But evening soon shall come with her shadow-woven
    shroud.

There never was a River without its mists of gray,
  There never was a Forest without its fallen leaf ;
And joy may walk beside us down the windings of our
    way,
  When lo ! there sounds a footstep, and we meet the
    face of Grief.

There never was a sea-shore without its drifting wreck,
  There never was an ocean without its moaning wave,
And the golden gleams of glory, the summer sky that
    fleck,
  Shine where dead stars are sleeping in their azure-
    mantled grave.

There never was a streamlet, however crystal clear,
    Without a shadow resting in the ripples of its tide,
Hope's brightest robes are broidered with the sable
        fringe of fear—
    And she lures us, but abysses girt her path on either
        side.

The shadow of the mountain falls athwart the lowly
        plain.
    And the shadow of the cloudlet hangs above the
        mountain's head—
And the highest hearts and lowest wear the shadow of
    some pain.
    And the smile has scarcely flitted ere the anguish'd
        tear is shed.

For no eyes have there been ever without a weary tear,
    And those lips cannot be human which have never
        heaved a sigh ;
For without the dreary winter there has never been a
    year,
    And the tempests hide their terrors in the calmest
        summer sky.

The cradle means the coffin, and the coffin means the
        grave ;
    The mother's song scarce hides the De Profundis of
        the Priest—
You may cull the fairest roses any May day ever gave,
    But they wither while you wear them ere the ending
        of your Feast.

So this dreary life is passing—and we move amid its
    maze,
    And we grope along together, half in darkness, half
        in light ;

And our hearts are often burdened by the mysteries of
our ways,
Which are never all in shadow and are never wholly
bright.

And our dim eyes ask a beacon, and our weary feet a
guide,
And our hearts of all life's mysteries seek the mean-
ing and the key ;
And a Cross gleams o'er our pathway, on it hangs the
Crucified,
And He answers all our yearnings by the whisper,
" Follow me."

Life is a Burden,—bear it ;
Life is a Duty,—dare it ;
Life is a thorn-crown,—wear it,
Though it break your heart in twain ;
Though the Burden crush you down.
Close your lips,—and hide your pain,
First the Cross – and then—the Crown.

IN ROME.

T last ; the dream of youth
   Stands fair and bright before me ;
The sunshine of the Home of Truth
   Falls tremulously o'er me.

And Tower and Spire and lofty Dome
   In brightest skies are gleaming ;—
Walk I, to-day, the ways of Rome ?
   Or am I only dreaming ?

No,—'tis no dream ;—my very eyes
   Gaze on the Hill-tops seven ;
Where crosses rise and kiss the skies
   And grandly point to Heaven.

Grey ruins loom on ev'ry side,
   Each stone an Age's story ;—
They seem the very ghosts of Pride
   That watch the grave of glory.

There senates sat, whose sceptre sought
   An empire without limit ;
There Grandeur dreamed its dream and thought
   That Death would never dim it.

There rulers reigned ;—yon heap of stones
   Was once their gorgeous palace ;
Beside them now, on altar-thrones,
   The priests lift up the chalice.

There legions marched with bucklers bright,
And lances lifted o'er them ;
While flags, like eagles plumed for flight,
Unfurled their wings before them.

There poets sang,—whose deathless name
Is linked to deathless verses ;
There heroes hushed with shouts of fame
Their trampled victims' curses.

There marched the warriors back to Home,
Beneath yon crumbling portal ;
And placed upon the brow of Rome
The proud crown of Immortal.

There soldiers stood with armor on
In steel-clad ranks and serried ;
The while their red swords flashed upon
The slaves whose rights they buried.

Here Pagan Pride, with sceptre, stood,
And Fame would not forsake it,—
Until a simple Cross of Wood
Came from the East to break it.

That Rome is dead,—here is the grave,—
Dead glory rises never,—
And countless Crosses o'er it wave
And will wave on forever.

Beyond the Tiber gleams a Dome
Above the Hill-tops seven ;—
It arches o'er the world from Rome
And leads the world to Heaven.

Dec. 6th, 1872.

AFTER SICKNESS.

I NEARLY died ;—I almost touched the Door
That swings between Forever and No-more ;
I think I heard the awful hinges grate,—
Hour after hour, while I did weary wait
Death's coming ;—but alas ! 'twas all in vain.
The Door half-opened and then closed again.

What were my thoughts ?   I had but one regret,
That I was doomed to live and linger yet
In this dark valley where the stream of tears
Flows,—and in flowing, deepens thro' the years.
My lips spake not,—my eyes were dull and dim,
But thro' my heart there moved a soundless hymn,-
A triumph-song of many chords and keys—
Transcending language,—as the summer breeze
Which, through the forest, mystically, floats,
Transcends the reach of mortal music's notes.
A song of victory,—a chant of bliss—
Wedded to words, it might have been like this ;—

"Come ! Death ! but I am fearless,
    I shrink not from your frown,—
The eyes you close are tearless,—
    Haste ! strike this frail form down.
Come ! there is no dissembling
    In this last, solemn hour,—
But you'll find my heart untrembling
    Before your awful power.
My lips grow pale and paler,

My eyes are strangely dim,
I wail not as a wailer,
   I sing a victor's hymn.
My limbs grow cold and colder,—
   My room is all in gloom,—
Bold Death!—but I am bolder—
   Come,—lead me to my tomb.
'Tis cold and damp and dreary,
   'Tis still and lone and deep,—
Haste, Death! my eyes are weary,
   I want to fall asleep.
Strike quick! Why dost thou tarry?
   Of time, why such a loss?
Dost fear the sign I carry?
   'Tis but a simple Cross.
Thou will not strike?—then hear me—
   Come! strike in any hour,—
My heart shall never fear thee
   Nor flinch before thy power.
I'll meet thee—Time's dread lictor—
   And my wasted lips shall sing :—
Dread Death!—I am the Victor—
   Strong Death! where is thy sting?'"

MILAN, Jan., 1873.

AFTER SEEING PIUS IX.

I SAW his face to-day ;—he looks a chief
    Who fears nor human rage, nor human guile ;
Upon his cheeks the twilight of a grief,
    But in that grief the starlight of a smile.
Deep, gentle eyes, with drooping lids that tell
They are the homes where tears of sorrow dwell ;
A low voice—strangely sweet—whose very tone
Tells how these lips speak oft with God alone.
I kissed his hand,—I fain would kiss his feet—
" No,—No ;" he said—and then in accents sweet
His blessing fell upon my bended head,—
He bade me rise ;—a few more words he said,
Then took me by the hand—the while he smiled—
And, going, whispered :—" Pray for me, my child."

SENTINEL SONGS.

WHEN falls the soldier brave
 Dead—at the feet of wrong,—
The poet sings—and guards his grave
 With sentinels of song.

Songs ! march ! he gives command,
 Keep faithful watch and true ;
The living and dead of the Conquered Land
 Have now no guards, save you.

Gray Ballads ! mark ye well !
 Thrice holy is your trust !
Go ! halt ! by the fields where warriors fell,
 Rest arms ! and guard their dust.

List ! Songs ! your watch is long !
 The soldiers' guard was brief,
Whilst right is right, and wrong is wrong—
 Ye may not seek relief.

Go ! wearing the gray of grief !
 Go ! watch o'er the Dead in Gray !
Go guard the private and guard the chief,
 And sentinel their clay !

And the songs—in stately rhyme,
 And with softly sounding tread,
Go forth, to watch for a time—a time,
 Where sleep the Deathless Dead.

And the songs—like funeral dirge,
  In music soft and low,
Sing round the graves—whilst hot tears surge
  From hearts that are homes of woe.

What ! tho' no sculptured shaft
  Immortalize each brave ?
What tho' no monument epitaphed
  Be built above each grave ?

When marble wears away
  And monuments are dust,—
The songs that guard our soldiers' clay
  Will still fulfil their trust.

With lifted head, and steady tread,
  Like stars that guard the skies,
Go watch each bed, where rest the dead,
  Brave songs ! with sleepless eyes.

*   *   *   *   *   *

When falls the cause of Right,
  The poet grasps his pen
And in gleaming letters of living light
  Transmits the Truth to men.

Go, Songs ! he says, who sings,
  Go ! tell the world this tale,—
Bear it afar on your tireless wings,
  The Right will yet prevail.

Songs ! sound ! like the thunder's breath !
  Boom o'er the world—and say,
Brave men may die,—Right has no death,
  Truth never shall pass away!

Go! sing! thro' a nation's sighs—
  Go! sob! thro' a people's tears!
Sweep the horizons of all the skies,
  And throb through a thousand years!

  *   *   *   *

And the songs, with brave, sad face,
  Go proudly down their way—
Wailing the loss of a conquered race,
  And waiting—an Easter-day.—

Away, away! like the birds,
  They soar in their flight sublime;
And the waving wings of the poet's words
  Flash down to the end of time.

When the Flag of Justice fails,
  Ere its folds have yet been furled,
The poet waves its folds in wails
  That flutter o'er the world.

Songs, march! and in rank by rank
  The low, wild verses go,
To watch the graves, where the grass is dank,
  And the martyrs sleep below.

Songs, halt! where there is no name,
  Songs, stay! where there is no stone,
And wait till you hear the feet of Fame
  Coming to where ye moan.

And the songs—with lips that mourn
  And with hearts that break in twain,
At the beck of the bard—a hope forlorn
  Watch the plain where sleep the slain.

When the warrior's sword is lowered,
  Ere its stainless sheen grows dim
The bard flings forth its dying gleam
  On the wings of a deathless hymn.

Songs, fly far o'er the world
  And adown to the end of time :—
Let the Sword still flash,—tho' its flag be furled,
  Thro' the sheen of the poet's rhyme.

Songs, fly as the eagles fly,
  The bard unbars the cage,
Go soar away—and afar and high
  Wave your wings o'er every age!

Shriek shrilly o'er each day,
  As future-ward ye fly,
That the men were right who wore the gray
  And Right can never die.

And the songs, with waving wing,
  Fly far—float far away
From the ages' crests, o'er the world they fling
  The shade of the stainless gray.

Might ! sing your triumph-songs !
  Each song but sounds a shame—
Go ! down the world, in loud-voiced throngs
  To win, from the future, fame.

Our ballads, born of tears,
  Will track you on your way,
And win the hearts of the future years
  For the men who wore the gray.

And so—say what you will,—
    In the heart of God's own laws
I have a faith, and my heart believes still
    In the triumph of our cause.

Such hope may all be vain
    And futile be such trust;
But the weary eyes that weep the slain,
    And watch above such dust—

They cannot help but lift
    Their visions to the skies,—
They watch the clouds—but wait the rift
    Through which their hope shall rise.

The victor wields the sword,
    Its blade may broken be,
By a thought that sleeps in a deathless word
    To wake in the Years—to be.

We wait a grand-voiced bard,
    Who when he sings—will send
Immortal songs' " Imperial Guard"
    The Lost cause to defend.

He has not come,—he will,—
    But when he chants—his song
Will stir the world to its depths, and thrill
    The earth with its tale of wrong.

The fallen cause still waits,—
    Its bard has not come yet,
His song—through one of to-morrow's gates
    Shall shine—but never set.

But when he comes—he'll sweep
    A harp with tears all-stringed,
And the very notes he strikes will weep,
    As they come, from his hand, woe-winged.

Ah ! grand shall be his strain,
    And his songs shall fill all climes,
And the Rebels shall rise and march again
    Down the lines of his glorious rhymes.

And through his verse shall gleam
    The swords that flashed in vain,
And the men who wore the gray shall seem
    To be marshalling again.

But hush ! between his words
    Peer faces sad and pale,
And you hear the sound of broken chords
    Beat through the poet's wail.

Through his verse the orphans cry—
    The terrible undertone !
And the father's curse and the mother's sigh,
    And the desolate young wife's moan.

      *   *   *   *   *

But harps are in every land
    That await a voice that sings,
And a maser-hand—but the humblest hand
    May gently touch its strings.

I sing with a voice too low
    To be heard beyond to-day,
In minor keys of my people's woe
    But my songs pass away.

To-morrow hears them not—
   To-morrow belongs to fame ·
My songs—like the birds'—will be forgot,
   And forgotten shall be my name.

And yet who knows ! betimes
   The grandest songs depart,
While the gentle, humble and low-toned rhymes
   Will echo from heart to heart.

But oh ! if in song or speech,
   In major or minor key,
My voice could over the ages reach
   I would whisper the name of Lee.

In the night of our defeat
   Star after star had gone,
But the way was bright to our soldiers' feet
   Where the star of Lee led on.

But sudden : there came a cloud,
   Out rung a nation's knell—
Our cause was wrapped in its winding shroud,
   All fell—when the great Lee fell.

From his men—with scarce a word,
   Silence ! when great hearts part !—·
But we know he sheathed his stainless sword
   In the wound of a broken heart.

He fled from Fame ;—but Fame
   Sought him in his retreat,
Demanding for the world one name
   Made deathless by defeat.

Nay! Fame! success is best!
  All lost! and nothing won—
North! keep the clouds that flush the West!
  We have the sinking sun.

All lost! but by the graves
  Where martyred heroes rest
He wins the most, who honor saves,
  Success is not the test.

All lost? a nation weeps ;—
  By all the tears that fall,
He loses naught who conscience keeps,
  Lee's honor saves us all.

All lost! but e'en defeat
  Hath triumphs of her own,
Wrong's pæan hath no note so sweet
  As trampled Right's proud moan.

The world shall yet decide,   .
  In truth's clear, far off light,
That the soldiers who wore the gray and died
  With Lee—were in the right.

And men, by time made wise,
  Shall in the future see
No name hath risen, or ever shall rise,
  Like the name of Robert Lee.

Ah me! my words are weak,
  This task surpasses me ;
Dead soldiers! rise from your graves and speak
  And tell how you loved Lee.

The banner you bore is furled,
  And the gray is faded, too !
But in all the colors that deck the world
  Your gray blends not with blue.

The colors are far apart,
  Graves sever them in twain ;
The Northern heart and the Southern heart
  May beat in peace again.

But still 'till Time's last day,
Whatever lips may plight,
  The Blue is Blue, but Gray is Gray,
Wrong never accords with Right.

Go ! Glory ! and forever guard
  Our chieftain's hallowed dust ;
And Honor ! keep eternal ward ;
  And Fame ! be this thy trust.

Go ! with your bright emblazoned scroll
  And tell the years to be—
The first of names that flash your roll
  Is ours—great Robert Lee.

Lee wore the gray ! since then
  'Tis Right's and Honor's hue !
He honored it, that man of men,
  And wrapped it round the True.

Dead ! but his spirit breathes,
  Dead ! but his heart is ours !
Dead ! but his sunny and sad land wreathes
  His crown with tears for flowers.

A Statue for his Tomb !—
  Mould it of marble white !
For Wrong, a spectre of Death and Doom ;
  An angel of Hope for Right.

But Lee has a thousand graves
  In a thousand hearts I ween ;
And tear drops fall from our eyes in waves
  That will keep his memory green.

Ah ! Muse ! you dare not claim
  A nobler man than he,
Nor nobler man hath less of blame,
Nor blameless man hath purer name,
Nor purer name hath grander fame,
  Nor Fame,—another Lee.

FRAGMENTS FROM AN EPIC POEM.

A MYSTERY.

face was sad ;—some shadow must have hung
Above his soul ;—its folds, now, falling dark,—
Now, almost bright ;—but dark or not so dark,
Like cloud upon a mount,—'twas always there—
A shadow ;—and his face was always sad.

His eyes were changeful,—for the gloom of gray
Within them met and blended with the blue,
And when they gazed they seemed almost to dream ;
They looked beyond you into far-away,
And often drooped ;—his face was always sad.

His eyes were deep ;—I often saw them dim,
As if the edges of a cloud of tears
Had gathered there, and only left a mist
That made them moist and kept them ever moist.
He never wept ;—his face was always sad.

I mean,—not many saw him ever weep,
And yet he seemed as one who often wept,
Or always, tears that were too proud to flow
In outer streams,—but shrunk within and froze,
Froze down into himself ; his face was sad.

And yet sometimes he smiled,—a sudden smile,
As if some far-gone joy came back again,
Surprised his heart, and flashed across his face
A moment,—like a light through rifts in clouds—·
Which falls upon an unforgotten grave ;
He rarely laughed ;—his face was ever sad.

And when he spoke his words were sad as wails,
And strange as stories of an unknown land,
And full of meanings as the sea of moans.
At times he was so still that silence seemed
To sentinel his lips ; and not a word
Would leave his heart;—his face was strangely sad.

But then at times his speech flowed like a stream—
A deep and dreamy stream through lonely dells
Of lofty mountain-thoughts, and o'er its waves
Hung mysteries of gloom,—and in its flow
It rippled on lone shores fair-fringed with flowers,
And deepened as it flowed ;—his face was sad.

He had his moods of silence and of speech.
I asked him once the reason—and he said :

" When I speak much—my words are only words,
When I speak least—my words are more than words,
When I speak not—I then reveal myself " !
It was his way of saying things,—he spoke
In quaintest riddles ; and his face was sad.

And when he wished, he wove around his words
A nameless spell that marvelously thrilled
The dullest ear.   'Twas strange that he so cold
Could warm the coldest heart ; that he so hard
Could soften hardest soul,—that he so still
Could rouse the stillest mind ;—his face was sad.

He spoke of death as if it were a toy
For thought to play with ; and of life he spoke
As of a toy not worth the play of thought ;
And of this world he spake as captives speak
Of prisons where they pine ; he spake of men
As one who found pure gold in each of them.
He spake of women—just as if he dreamed
About his mother ;—and he spoke of God
As if he walked with Him and knew His Heart—
But he was weary,—and his face was sad.

He had a weary way in all he did,
As if he dragged a chain, or bore a cross ;
And yet the weary went to him for rest.
His heart seemed scarce to know an earthly joy,   ·
And yet the joyless were rejoiced by him.
He seemed to have two selves,—his outer self
Was free to any passer by, and kind to all,
And gentle as a child's ; that outer self
Kept open all its gates that whoso wished
Might enter them and find therein a place :
And many entered ;—but his face was sad.

The inner self he guarded from approach,
He kept it sealed and sacred as a shrine ;
He guarded it with Silence and Reserve,
Its gates were locked and watched, and none might pass
Beyond the portals ;—and his face was sad.

But whoso entered there, and few were they,
So very few—so very—very few,
They never did forget ;—they said : "How strange "!
They murmured still, "How strange ! how strangely
   strange "!
They went their ways but wore a lifted look,
And higher meanings came to common words,
And lowly thoughts took on the grandest tones,—
And near or far—they never did forget
The "Shadow and the Shrine " ;—his face was sad.

He was nor young nor old,—yet he was both;—
Nor both by turns, but always both at once ;
For youth and age commingled in his ways,
His words, his feelings, and his thoughts and acts.
At times the "old man" tottered in his thoughts,—
The child played thro' his words ;—his face was sad.

I one day asked his age ; he smiled and said :
"The rose that sleeps upon yon valley's breast,
Just born to-day, is not as young as I ;
The moss-robed oak of twice a thousand storms,—
An acorn cradled ages long ago,—
Is old, in sooth, but not as old as I."
It was his way,—he always answered thus,—
But when he did, his face was very sad.

SPIRIT-SONG.

Thou wert once the purest wave
  Where the tempests roar ;—
Thou art now a golden wave
  On the golden shore—
    Ever—ever—Evermore !

Thou wert, once, the bluest wave
  Shadows e'er hung o'er ;—
Thou art now the brightest wave
  On the brightest shore—
    Ever—ever—Evermore !

Thou wert once the gentlest wave
  Ocean ever bore ;
Thou art now the fairest wave
  On the fairest shore,—
    Ever—ever—Evermore.

Whiter foam than thine oh ! wave !
  Wavelet never wore ;—
Stainless wave ; and now you lave
  The far and stormless shore,—
    Ever—ever—Evermore.

Who bade thee go ? oh ! bluest wave
  Beyond the tempest's roar ?
Who bade thee flow? oh ! fairest wave !
  Unto the golden shore ?
    Ever—ever—Evermore !

Who waved a hand ? oh ! purest wave !
  A hand that blessings bore ;—
And wafted thee,—oh ! whitest wave !
  Unto the fairest shore ?
    Ever—ever—Evermore !

Who winged thy way? oh! holy wave!
  In days and days of yore?
And wept the words? "Oh! winsome wave!
  This earth is not thy shore?"
    Ever—ever—Evermore!

Who gave thee strength? oh! snowy wave!
  The strength a great soul wore—
And said: "Float up to God! my wave!
  His heart shall be thy shore"!
    Ever—ever—Evermore!

Who said to thee? oh! poor, weak wave!
  "Thy wail shall soon be o'er,
Float on to God,—and leave me, wave,
  Upon this rugged shore"!
    Ever—ever—Evermore!

And thou hast reached His feet,—glad wave!
  Dos't dream of days of yore?
Dos't yearn that we shall meet,—pure wave,
  Upon the golden shore?
    Ever—ever—Evermore!

Thou sleepest in the calm;—calm wave!
  Beyond the wild storm's roar!
I watch amid the storm;—bright wave,
  Like Rock upon the shore;—
    Ever—ever—Evermore!

Sing at the feet of God, white wave!
  Song sweet as one of yore;
I would not bring thee back, Heart-wave,
  To break upon this shore,—
    Ever—ever—Evermore!

*   *   *   *   *   *

—" No—no,—" he gently spoke,—"you know me not;—
My mind is like a Temple, dim, vast,—lone,—
Just like a Temple, when the Priest is gone,—
And all the hymns that rolled along the vaults
Are buried deep in Silence ; when the lights
That flashed on altars died away in Dark,
And when the flowers, with all their perfumed breath
And beauteous bloom, lie withered on the shrine.
My mind is like a Temple, solemn, still,
Untenanted save by the ghosts of gloom
Which seem to linger in the Holy-place—
The shadows of the sinners, who passed there,
And wept and Spirit-shriven left upon
The marble floor memorials of their tears."

And while he spake, his words sank low and low,—
Until they hid themselves in some still depth
He would not open,—and his face was sad.

When he spoke thus, his very gentleness
Passed slowly from him,—and his look so mild
Grew marble cold ;—a pallor as of death
Whitened his lips,—and clouds rose to his eyes,—
Dry, rainless clouds, where lightnings seemed to sleep.
His words, as tender as a rose's smile,
Slow-hardened into thorns,—but seemed to sting
Himself the most ;—-his brow, at such times, bent
Most lowly down,—and wore such look of pain
As though it bore an unseen crown of thorns.—
Who knows, perhaps, it did !

                    But he would pass
His hand upon his brow,—or touch his eyes,
And then the olden gentleness, like light

Which seems transfigured by the touch of Dark,
Would tremble on his face,—and he would look
More gentle then than ever,—and his tone
Would sweeten, like the winds, when storms have passed.

I saw him, one day, thus most deeply moved
And darkened ;—ah ! his face was like a tomb
That hid the dust of dead and buried smiles,—
But, suddenly, his face flashed like a throne,
And all the smiles arose as from the dead,
And wore the glory of an Easter-morn ;—
And passed beneath the sceptre of a Hope
Which came from some far-region of his heart,—
Came up into his eyes,—and reigned a queen.
I marveled much,—he answered to my look
With all his own,—and wafted me these words :

"There are transitions in the lives of all.
There are transcendant moments when we stand
In Thabor's glory with the Chosen Three,
And weak with very strength of human love
We fain would build our Tabernacles there ;—
And Peter-like, for very human joy,
We cry aloud—''tis good that we are here':
Swift are these moments, like the smile of God
Which glorifies a Shadow,—and is gone.

And then we stand upon another mount,—
Dark, rugged Calvary;—and God keeps us there
For awful hours,—to make us there his own
In Crucifixion's tortures,—'tis his way.
We wish to cling to Thabor ;—He says : "No."
And what he says is best because most true.
We fain would fly from Calvary;—He says : "No."

And it is true because it is the best.
And yet, my friend, these two mounts are the same.

They lie apart, distinct and separate,—
And yet—strange mystery !—they are the same.
For Calvary is a Thabor in the Dark,
And Thabor is a Calvary in the Light.
It is the Mystery of Holy Christ !
It is the mystery of you and me !
Earth's shadows move, as moves far-Heaven's sun,
And like the shadows of a Dial, we
Tell, darkly, in the Vale the very hours
The sun tells, brightly, in the sinless skies.
Dost understand ?"   I did not understand,—
Or only half ;—his face was very sad.
" Dost thou not understand me?   Then your life
Is shallow as a brook that brawls along
Between two narrow shores ;—you never wept,—
You never wore great clouds upon your brow
As mountains wear them ;—and you never wore
Strange glories in your eyes, as sunset-skies·
Oft wear them,—and your lips,—they never sighed
Grand sighs which bear the weight of all the soul ;
You never reached your arms a-broad,—a-high
To grasp far-worlds—or to enclasp the sky.
Life, only life can understand a life ;—
Depth,—only depth can understand the deep.
The dewdrop glist'ning on the lily's face
Can never learn the story of the sea.

＊　　＊　　＊　　＊　　＊　　＊

One day we strolled together to the sea.
Gray-Evening and the Night had almost met,—
We walked between them,—silent, to the shore.

The feet of weird-faced waves ran up the beach
Like children in mad play,—then back again,—
As if the Spirit of the land pursued,—
Then up again,—and farther—and they flung
White, foamy arms around each other's neck,—
Then back again with sudden rush and shout,
As if the sea, their mother, called them home ;—
Then leaned upon her breast, as if so tired,
But swiftly tore themselves away and rushed
Away,—and further up the beach and fell
For utter weariness ;—and loudly sobbed
For strength to rise and flow back to the Deep.—
But all in vain,—for other waves swept on
And trampled them ;—the sea cried out in grief,—
The gray beach laughed, and clasped them to the sands.
It was the Flood-tide and the Even-tide—
Between the Evening and the Night we walked,—
We walked between the billows and the beach,—
We walked between the Future and the Past,—
Down to the sea, we, twain, had strolled,—to part.

The shore was low, with just the faintest rise
Of many-colored sands and shreds of shells,
Until about a stone's far throw they met,
A fringe of faded grass, with here and there
A pale-green shrub ; and farther into land—
Another stone's throw farther, there were trees,
Tall, dark, wild trees, with intertwining arms,
Each almost touching each, as if they feared
To stand alone and look upon the sea.
The Night was in the trees—the Evening, on the shore.
We walked between the Evening and the Night,—
Between the trees and tide we silent strolled.

There lies between man's Silence and his Speech
A shadowy valley where thro' those, who pass
Are never silent tho' they may not speak,—
And yet they more than breathe ;—it is the Vale
Of wordless sighs, half-uttered and half-heard,—
It is the vale of the Unutterable.
We walked between our Silence and our Speech.
And sighed between the sunset and the stars,
One hour beside the sea.

There was a cloud
Far o'er the reach of waters hanging low
'Tween sea and sky,—the banner of the storm.
Its edges faintly bright, as if the rays,
That fled far down the West, had rested there
And slumbered,—and had left a dream of light.
Its inner folds were dark, —its central, more.
It did not flutter,—there it hung as calm
As banner in a temple o'er a shrine.
Its shadow only fell upon the sea,
Above the shore the heavens bended blue.
We walked between the Cloudless and the Cloud,
That hour, beside the sea.

But, quick as thought,
There gleamed a sword of wild, terrific light,
Its hilt in heaven,—its point hissed in the sea,—
Its scabbard in the darkness,—and it tore
The bannered cloud into a thousand shreds,
Then quivered far away,—and bent and broke
In flashing fragments ;—

And there came a peal
That shook the mighty sea from shore to shore,
But did not stir a sand-grain on the beach ;

Then silence fell,—and where the low cloud hung,
Clouds darker gathered—and they proudly waved
Like flags before a battle.—

          We, twain, walked,—
We walked between the lightning's parted gleams,
We walked between the thunders of the skies,
We walked between the wavings of the clouds,
We walked between the tremblings of the sea,
We walked between the stillnesses and roars
Of frightened billows;—and we walked between
The coming tempest and the dying calm,
Between the Tranquil and the Terrible,
That hour, beside the sea.

          There was a Rock,
Far up the winding beach, that jutted in
The sea,—and broke the heart of every wave
That struck its breast;—not steep enough nor high
To be a cliff,—nor yet sufficient rough
To be a crag; a simple, low, lone Rock;—
Yet not so low as that its brow was laved
By highest tide,—yet not sufficient high
To rise beyond the reach of silver-spray
That rained up from the waves,—their tears that fell
Upon its face, when they died at his feet.
Around its sides damp sea-weed hung in long,
Sad tresses, dripping down into the sea.
A tuft or two of grass did green the Rock,
A patch or so of moss;—the rest was bare.

Adown the shore we walked 'tween Eve and Night;
But when we reached the Rock, the Eve and Night
Had met;—light died; we sat down in the Dark
Upon the Rock.

          Meantime a thousand clouds
Careered and clashed in air,—a thousand waves
Whirled wildly on in wrath,—a thousand winds
Howled hoarsely on the main ;—and down the skies
Into the hollow seas the fierce rain rushed,
As if its ev'ry drop were hot with wrath ;
And like a thousand serpents intercoiled
The lightnings glared and hissed and hissed and glared,
And all the horror shrank in horror back
Before the maddest peals that ever leaped
Out from the thunder's throat.
                    Within the dark
We silent sat.   No rain fell on the Rock,
Nor in on land, nor shore ;—only on sea
The upper and the lower waters met
In wild delirium,—like a thousand hearts
Far-parted,—parted-long, which meet to break,.
Which rush into each other's arms and break
In terror and in tempests wild of tears.
No rain fell on the rock ;—but flakes of foam
Swept cold against our faces, where we sat
Between the hush and howling of the winds,
Between the swells and sinkings of the waves,
Between the stormy sea and stilly shore,
Between the rushings of the maddened rains,
Between the Dark beneath and Dark above.

We sat within the dread Heart of the Night—
One, pale with terror ;—One, as calm and still
And stern and moveless as the lone, low Rock.

     *   *   *   *   *   *

LAKE COMO.

WINTER on the mountains—
 Summer on the shore—
The robes of sun-gleams woven,
 The lake's blue wavelets roar.

Cold, white, against the Heavens,
 Flashed winter's crown of snow,
And the blossoms of the spring-tide
 Waved brightly far below.

The mountain's head was dreary,
 The cold and cloud were there,
But the mountain's feet were sandaled,
 With flowers of beauty rare.

And winding thro' the mountains,
 The lake's calm wavelets rolled ;
And a cloudless sun was gilding,
 Their ripples with its gold.

Adown the lake we glided,
 Thro' all the sunlit day ;
The cold snows gleamed above us,
 But fair flowers fringed our way.

The snows crept down the mountain,
 The flowers crept up the slope,
Till they seemed to meet and mingle,
 Like a human, fear and hope.

But the same rich golden sunlight,
  Fell on the flowers and snow;
Like the smile of God that flashes,
  On hearts in joy or woe.

And on the lake's low margin,
  The trees wore stoles of green;
While here and there, amid them,
  A convent cross was seen.

Anon a ruined castle,
  Moss-mantled, loomed in view,
And cast its solemn shadow,
  Across the water's blue.

And chapel, cot and villa,
  Met here and there our gaze;
And many a crumbling tower,
  That told of other days.

And scattered o'er the waters,
  The fishing boats lay still;
And sound of song, so softly,
  Came echoed from the hill

At times the mountains shadow,
  Fell dark across the scene;
And veiled with veil of purple,
  The wavelets' silver sheen.

But for a moment only,
  The lake would wind,—and lo!
The waves would near the glory,
  Of the sunlight's brightest glow.

At times, there fell a silence,
  Unbroken by a tone ;
As if no sound of voices,
  Had ever there been known.

Through strange and lonely places,
  We glided thus for hours ;
We saw no other faces
  But the faces of the flowers.

The shores were sad and lonely,
  As hearts without a love ;
While darker and more dreary,
  The mountains rose above.

But sudden round a headland,
  The lake would sweep again ;
And voices from a village,
  Would meet us with their strain.

Thus all the day we glided,
  Until the Vesper bell,
Gave to the day, at sunset,
  Its sweet and soft farewell.

Then back again we glided,
  Upon our homeward way;
When twilight wrapped the waters
  And the mountains with its gray

But, brief the reign of twilight,
  The night came quickly on ;
The dark brow o'er the mountains
  Star wreathed brightly shone.

And down thro' all the shadows,
　　The star-gleams softly crept,
And kissed with lips all-shining,
　　The wavelets ere they slept.

The lake lay in a slumber,
　　The shadows for its screen;
While silence waved her sceptre,
　　Above the sleeping scene.

The spirit of the darkness,
　　Moved ghost-like everywhere;
Wherever starlight glimmered,
　　Its shadow, sure, fell there.

The lone place grew more lonely,
　　And all along our way,
The mysteries of the night-time,
　　Held undisputed sway.

Thro' silence and thro' darkness
　　We glided down the tide—
That wound around the mountains
　　That rose on either side.

No eyes would close in slumber
　　Within our little bark—
What charmed us so in daylight
　　So awed us in the dark.

Upon the deck we lingered
　　A whisper scarce was heard;
When hearts are stirred profoundest
　　Lips are without a word.

"Let's say the Chaplet," softly
  A voice beside me spake.
"Christ walked once in the darkness
  Across an Eastern lake."

"And to-night we know the secret
  That will charm him to our side;
If we call upon His Mother—
  He will meet us on the tide."

So we said the Beads together
  Up and down the little bark,
And I believe that Jesus met us
  With His Mother in the dark.

And our prayers were scarcely ended
  When on mountain top afar,
We beheld the morning meeting
  With the night's last fading star.

And I left the lake—but never
  Shall the years to come efface
From my heart the dream and vision
  Of that strange and lonely place.

Feb. 1st, 1873.

"PEACE! BE STILL."

SOMETIMES the Saviour sleeps,—and it is dark,—
  For oh! His eyes are this world's only light;—
And when they close wild waves rush on His Bark
  And toss it through the dread hours of the Night.

So He slept once upon an Eastern lake,
  In Peter's bark, while wild waves raved at will;
A cry smote on him,—and when he did wake
  He softly whispered,—and the sea grew still.

It is a mystery,—but He seems to sleep
  As erst he slept in Peter's wave-rocked bark:
A storm is sweeping all across the deep,
  While Pius prays, like Peter, in the Dark.

The sky is darkened,—and the shore is far,
  The tempest's strength grows fiercer every hour;
Upon the howling deep there shines no star—
  Why sleeps he still? Why does he hide his power?

Fear not—a holy hand is on the helm
  That guides the bark thro' all the tempest's wrath;
Quail not,—the wildest waves can never whelm
  The ship of Faith upon its homeward path.

The Master sleeps,—His Pilot guards the Bark,
  He soon will wake; and at his mighty will
The Light will shine where all before was dark,—
  The wild waves still remember: "Peace! be still."

Rome, 1873.

GOOD FRIDAY.

H! Heart! of Three-in-the Evening!
  You nestled the thorn-crowned Head,
He leaned on you in His sorrow,
  And rested on you when dead.

Ah! Holy Three-in-the Evening!
  He gave you His richest dower—
He met you afar on Calvary,
  · And made you " His own last Hour."

Oh! Brow of Three-in-the Evening,
  Thou wearest a crimson crown ;
Thou art Priest of the Hours forever,
  And thy voice as thou goest down

The cycles of Time, still murmurs
  The story of love, each day ;
"I held, in death, the Eternal
  In the long and the far-away.

Oh! Heart of Three-in-the Evening!
  Mine beats with thine to-day ;
Thou tellest the olden story,
  I kneel—and I weep and pray.

Boulogne, sur mer.

SUNLESS DAYS.

THEY come to ev'ry life,—sad, sunless days,
    With not a light all o'er their clouded skies—
And thro' the Dark we grope along our ways,
    With hearts fear-filled, and lips low-breathing sighs.

What is the Dark?—Why cometh it? and whence?
    Why does it banish all the Bright away?
How does it weave a spell o'er soul and sense?
    Why falls the Shadow where'er gleams the Ray?

Has't felt it? I have felt it, and I know,—
. How oft and suddenly the shadows roll
From out the depths of some dim realm of woe,—
    To wrap their darkness round the human soul.

Those days are darker than the very night;
    For nights have stars, and sleep and happy dreams,
But these days bring unto the spirit-sight
    The mysteries of gloom,—until it seems

The light is gone forever, and the Dark
    Hangs like a pall of death above the soul
Which rocks amid the gloom like storm-swept bark
    And sinks beneath a sea where tempests roll.

Winter on the Atlantic.

A REVERIE.

DID I dream of a song? or sing in a dream?
Why ask when the night only knoweth?
The night,—and the Angel of Sleep!
But ever since then, a music deep,
Like a stream thro' a shadow-land floweth
Under each thought of my spirit that groweth
Into the blossom and bloom of speech,—
Under each fancy that cometh and goeth
Wayward, as waves when Evening-breeze bloweth
Out of the sunset and into the beach.
And is it a wonder I wept to-day?
For I mused and thought,—but I cannot say
If I dreamed of a song,—or sang in a dream.
In the silence of sleep,—and the noon of night;
And now—even now—'neath the words I write,
The flush of the dream, or the flow of the song—
I cannot tell which—moves strangely along.
But why write more? I am puzzled sore:
Did I dream of a song? or sing in a dream?
Ah! hush! heart! hush!—'tis of no avail,
The words of earth are a darksome veil,
The poet weaves it with artful grace;
Lifts it off from his thoughts at times,
Lets it rustle along his rhymes,—
But gathers it close, covering the face
Of ev'ry thought that must not part
From out the keeping of his heart.

MY BEADS.

SWEET, Blessed Beads! I would not part
    With one of you, for richest gem
    That gleams in kingly diadem ;—
Ye know the history of my heart.

For I have told you every grief
    In all the days of twenty years,
    And I have moistened you with tears,
And in your decades found relief.

Ah ! time has fled, and friends have failed,
    And joys have died ;—but in my needs,
    Ye were my friends ! my Blessed Beads !
And ye consoled me when I wailed.

For many and many a time in grief,
    My weary fingers wandered round
    Thy circled- hain, and always found
In some Hail-Mary sweet relief.

How many a story you might tell
    Of inner-life to all unknown,—
    I trusted you and you alone,—
But ah ! ye keep my secrets well.

Ye are the only chain I wear,
    A sign that I am but the slave,
    In life, in death, beyond the grave,
Of Jesus and His Mother fair.

AT NIGHT.

REARY! weary!
Weary! dreary!
Sighs my soul this lonely night.
Farewell gladness!
Welcome sadness!
Vanished are my visions bright!

Stars are shining!
Winds are pining!
In the sky and o'er the sea;
Shine forever
Stars; but never
Can the starlight gladden me.

Stars! you nightly
Sparkle brightly,
Scattered o'er your azure dome,
While earth's turning,
There you're burning—
Beacons of a better home.

Stars! you brighten
And you lighten
Many a heart-grief here below:
But your gleaming,
And your beaming,
Cannot chase away my woe.

Stars ! you're shining—
I am pining—
I am dark, but you are bright;
Hanging o'er me
And before me
Is a night you cannot light.

Night of sorrow,
Whose to-morrow
I may never, never see,
Till upon me
And around me
Dawns a bright eternity.

Winds ! you're sighing,
And you're crying,
Like a mourner o'er a tomb :
Whither go ye?
Whither blow ye?
Wailing through the midnight gloom.

Chanting lowly,
Softly, lowly,
Like the voice of one in woe :
Winds so lonely,
Why thus moan ye?
Say, what makes you sorrow so?

Are you grieving
For your leaving
Scenes where all is fair and gay?
For the flowers
In their bowers
You have met with on your way?

For fond faces,
For dear places,
That you've seen as on you swept.
Are you sighing?
Are you crying?
O'er the memories they have left?

Earth is sleeping
While you're sweeping
Through night solemn silence by!
On forever,
Pausing never—
How I love to hear you sigh!

Men are dreaming,
Stars are gleaming,
In the far-off heaven's blue;
Bosom aching,
Musing, waking,
Midnight winds! I sigh with you!

NOCTURNE.

ETIMES, I seem to see in dreams
What when awake I may not see;
Can Night be God's more than the Day?
Do stars, not suns' best light His way?
Who knoweth? Blended lights and shades
Arch aisles down which He walks to me.

I hear Him coming in the Night
  Afar, and yet I know not how,
    His steps make music low and sweet—
    Sometimes the Nails are in His feet ;
Does Darkness give God better light
  Than Day—to find a weary brow ?

Does Darkness give man brighter rays
  To find the God, in Sunshine lost ?
    Must shadows wrap the Trysting-place
    Where God meets hearts with gentlest grace ?
Who knoweth it ? God hath his ways
  For every soul here sorrow-tossed.

The Hours of Day are like the waves
  That fret against the shores of sin,
    They touch the Human everywhere,
    The Bright-Divine fades in their glare ;
And God's sweet voice the spirit craves
  Is heard too faintly in the din.

When all the senses are awake,
  The Mortal presses overmuch
    Upon the great Immortal part—•
    And God seems further from the Heart.
Must souls, like skies, when day-dawns break,
  Lose star by star at sunlight's touch ?

But when the sun kneels in the west,
  And grandly sinks as great Hearts sink ;
    And in his sinking, flings adown
    Bright blessings from his fading crown,
The stars begin their Song of Rest,
  And shadows make the thoughtless think.

The Human seems to fade away—
  And down the starred and shadowed skies
    The Heavenly comes—as memories come
    Of Home ; to hearts afar from Home ;
  And thro' the Darkness after Day
    Many a winged angel flies.

And, somehow, tho' the eyes see less,
  Our spirits seem to see the more—
    When we look thro' Night's shadow-bars
    The soul sees more than shining stars,
Yea—sees the very loveliness
  That rests upon the " Golden Shore."

Strange Reveries steal o'er us then
  Like keyless chords of instruments,
    With music's soul without the notes ;
    And subtle, sad, and sweet there floats
A melody not made by men—
  Nor ever heard by outer sense.

And " what has been," and " what will be,"
  And " what is not, but might have been,"—
    The dim " to be "—the " mournful gone,"
    The little things life rested on
In " Long-ago's," give tone, not key
  To reveries beyond our ken.

ST. MARY'S.

BACK to where the roses rest
Round a shrine of holy name—
(Yes—they knew me when I came)—
More of peace and less of fame
    Suit my restless heart the best.

Back to where long quiets brood,
Where the calm is never stirred
By the harshness of a word—
But instead the singing bird
    Sweetens all my solitude.

With the birds and with the flowers
Songs and silences unite,—
From the morning unto night,
And somehow a clearer light
    Shines along the quiet hours.

God comes closer to me here,—
Back of ev'ry rose leaf there
He is hiding,—and the air
Thrills with calls to holy prayer ;
    Earth grows far,—and heaven near.

Every single flower is fraught
With the very sweetest dreams,
Under clouds or under gleams
Changeful ever,—yet meseems
    On each leaf I read God's thought.

Still, at times, as place of death,—
Not a sound to vex the ear,
Yet withal it is not drear,—
Better for the heart to hear
   Far from men—God's gentle breath.

Where men clash, God always clings,-
When the human passes by,
Like a cloud from summer sky
God so gently draweth nigh,
   And the brightest blessings brings.

List ! e'en now a wild bird sings
And the roses seem to hear,
Every note that thrills my ear
Rising to the heavens clear
   And my soul soars on its wings.

Up into the silent skies   ·
Where the sunbeams veil the star,
Up—beyond the clouds afar,
Where no discords ever mar,
   Where rests peace that never dies.

So I live within the calm,
And the birds and roses know
That the days that come and go
Are as peaceful as the flow
   Or a prayer beneath a psalm.

DE PROFUNDIS.

H ! Days so dark with Death's eclipse!
　　Woe are we! woe are we!
　And the Nights are Ages long,—
From breaking hearts, thro' pallid lips
　　Oh, my God ! woe are we !
　Trembleth the mourners' song,—
　　A blight is falling on the fair
　　And Hope is dying in despair,—
　　And Terror walketh everywhere.

All the hours are full of tears,—
　　Oh. my God! woe are we!
　Grief keeps watch in brightest eyes—·
Every heart is strung with fears,
　　Woe are we ! woe are we !
　All the light hath left the skies,
　　And the living awe-struck crowds
　　See above them only clouds
　　And around them only shrouds.

Ah ! the terrible Farewells !
　　Woe are they ! woe are they!
　When last words sink into moans,
While life's trembling vesper bells
　　Oh, my God ! woe are we !
　Ring the awful undertones !
　　Not a sun in any day !
　　In the night-time not a ray,—
　　And the dying pass away !

Dark! so dark! above—below,—
　　Oh, my God! woe are we!
　　Cowereth every human life.—
Wild the wailing;—to and fro—
　　Woe are all! woe are we!
　　Death is victor in the strife:—
　　　In the hut and in the hall
　　　He is writing on the wall
　　　Dooms for many—fears for all.

Thro' the cities burns a breath,
　　Woe are they! woe are we!
　　Hot with dread and deadly wrath;
Life and Love lock arms in death,
　　Woe are they! woe are all!
　　Victims strew the Spectre's path;
　　　Shy-eyed children softly creep
　　　Where their mothers wail and weep—
　　　In the grave their fathers sleep.

Mothers waft their prayers on high,—
　　Oh, my God! woe are we!
　　With their dead child on their breast.
And the Altars ask the sky,—
　　Oh, my Christ! woe are we!
　　"Give the dead, oh, Father! rest!
　　　Spare thy people! mercy! spare!"
　　　Answer will not come to prayer—
　　　Horror moveth everywhere.

And the Temples miss the Priest—
　　Oh, my God! woe are we!
　　And the cradle mourns the child.
Husband! at your bridal feast
　　Woe are you! woe are you!

Think how those poor dead eyes smiled;
    They will never smile again—
    Every tie is cut in twain,
    All the strength of love is vain.

Weep? but tears are weak as foam—
    Woe are ye! woe are we!
They but break upon the shore
Winding between Here and Home—
    Woe are ye! woe are we!
Wailing never—nevermore!
    Ah, the dead! they are so lone,
    Just a grave, and just a stone,
    And the memory of a moan.

Pray? yes, pray, for God is sweet—
    Oh, my God! woe are we!
Tears will trickle into prayers
When we kneel down at His feet—
    Woe are we! woe are we!
With our crosses and our cares.
    He will calm the totured breast,
    He will give the troubled rest—
    And the dead He watcheth best.

WHEN?

SOME day in Spring
   When earth is fair and glad
And sweet birds sing
   And fewest hearts are sad—
   Shall I die then?
   Ah! me! no matter when,
I know it will be sweet
   To leave the homes of men
And rest beneath the sod,
To kneel and kiss Thy feet
   In Thy Home! Oh! my God.

Some Summer morn
   Of splendors and of songs,
When roses hide the thorn
   And smile,—the spirit's wrongs—·
   Shall I die then?
   Ah! me! no matter when,
I know I will rejoice
   To leave the haunts of men
And lie beneath the sod,
To hear Thy tender voice
   In Thy Home! Oh! my God.

Some Autumn eve
  When chill clouds drape the sky,·
When bright things grieve
  Because all fair things die,—
    Shall I die then?
    Ah ! me ! no matter when,
I know I shall be glad
    Away from the homes of men,
  Adown beneath the sod,
My heart will not be sad
  In Thy Home ! Oh ! my God.

Some Wintry day
  When all skies wear a gloom,
And beauteous May
  Sleeps in December's tomb,—
    Shall I die then ?
    Ah ! me ! no matter when,
My soul shall throb with joy
    To leave the haunts of men
  And sleep beneath the sod,—
Ah ! there is no alloy
  In Thy joys ! Oh ! my God.

Haste, Death ! be fleet,
I know it will be sweet
  To rest beneath the sod,—
To kneel and kiss Thy feet
  In heaven, Oh ! my God.

THE CONQUERED BANNER.

FURL that Banner, for 'tis weary;
Round its staff 'tis drooping dreary;
  Furl it, fold it, it is best :
For there's not a man to wave it,
And there' not a sword to save it,
And there's not one left to lave it
In the blood which heroes gave it;
And its foes now scorn and brave it;
  Furl it, hide it—let it rest.

Take that Banner down, 'tis tattered;
Broken is its staff and shattered;
And the valiant hosts are scattered,
  Over whom it floated high.
Oh ! 'tis hard for us to fold it;
Hard to think there's none to hold it;
Hard that those, who once unrolled it,
  Now must furl it with a sigh.

Furl that Banner—furl it sadly;
Once ten thousands hailed it gladly,
And ten thousands wildly, madly,
  Swore it should forever wave ;
Swore that foeman's sword should never
Hearts like theirs entwined dissever,
Till that flag should float forever
  O'er their freedom, or their grave !

FOR THE BANNER TAKES. . .
TO MEET THE WARRIORS.

THE CONQUERED BANNER.

Furl it! for the hands that grasped it,
And the hearts that fondly clasped it,
  Cold and dead are lying low ;
And that Banner—it is trailing !
While around it sounds the wailing
  Of its people in their woe.

For, though conquered, they adore it !
Love the cold, dead hands that bore it !
Weep for those who fell before it !
Pardon those who trailed and tore it !
But, oh ! wildly they deplore it,
  Now who furl and fold it so.

Furl that Banner ! True. 'tis gory,
Yet 'tis wreathed around with glory,
And 'twill live in song and story,
  Though its folds are in the dust :
For its fame on brightest pages,
Penned by poets and by sages,
Shall go sounding down the ages—
  Furl its folds though now we must.

Furl that Banner, softly, slowly,
Treat it gently—it is holy—
  For it droops above the dead.
Touch it not—unfold it never,
Let it droop there, furled forever,
  For its people's hopes are dead !

A CHRISTMAS CHAUNT.

HEY ask me to sing them a Christmas song,
    That with musical mirth shall ring;
How know I that the world's great throng
    Will care for the words I sing?

Let the young and the gay chaunt the Christmas lay,
    Their voices and hearts are glad ;
But I—I am old, and my locks are gray,
    And they tell me my voice is sad.

Ah ! once I could sing, when my heart beat warm
    With hopes, bright as Life's first spring ;
But the Spring hath fled, and the golden charm
    Hath gone from the songs I sing.

I have lost the spell that my verse could weave
    O'er the souls of the old and young ;
And never again—how it makes me grieve—
    Shall I sing as once I sung.

Why ask a song ? ah ! perchance you believe,
    Since my days are so nearly past,
That the song you'll hear on this Christmas Eve,
    Is the old man's best and last.

Do you want the jingle of rhythm and rhyme ?
    Art's sweet but meaningless notes,
Or the music of Thought ? that, like the chime
    Of a grand Cathedral , floats.

Out of each word, and along each line,
    Into the spirit's ear,
Lifting it up, and making it pine,
    For a Something far from Here:

Bearing the wings of the soul aloft
    From earth and its shadows dim;
Soothing the breast with a sound as soft
    As a dream, or a Seraph's hymn;

Evoking the solemnest hopes and fears
    From our Being's higher part,
Dimming the eyes with radiant tears
    That flow from a spell-bound heart.

Do they want a song that is only a song,
    With no mystical meanings rife?
Or a music that solemnly moves along—
    The undertone of a life?

Well, then, I'll sing; though I know no art,
    Nor the Poet's rhymes nor rules—
A melody moves through my aged heart
    Not learned from the books or schools:

A music I learned in the days long gone—
    I cannot tell where or how—
But no matter where, it still sounds on
    Back of this wrinkled brow;

And down in my heart I hear it still,
    Like the echoes of far-off bells;
Like the dreamy sound of a Summer rill
    Flowing through fairy dells.

But what shall I sing for the world's gay throng,
And what the words of the old man's song?

The world, they tell me, is so giddy grown,
    That Thought is rare :
And thoughtless minds and shallow hearts alone
    Hold empire there ;

That fools have prestige, place, and power, and fame,
    Can it be true?
That wisdom is a scorn, a hissing shame,
    And wise are few?

They tell me, too, that all is venal, vain,
    With high and low ;
That Truth and Honor are the slaves of Gain ;
    Can it be so?

That lofty Principle hath long been dead
    And in a shroud :
That Virtue walks ashamed, with downcast head,
    Amid the crowd.

They tell me, too, that few they are who own
    God's Law and Love ;
That thousands, living for this earth alone,
    Look not above ;

That daily, hourly, from the bad to worse,
    Men tread the path,
Blaspheming God, and careless of the curse
    Of His dread wrath.

And must I sing for slaves of sordid gain,—
    Or to the Few
Shall I not dedicate this Christmas strain
    Who still are true?

1   No—not for the False shall I strike the strings
      Of the lyre that was mute so long;
If I sing at all—the gray bard sings
      For the Few and the True his song.

And ah ! there is many a changeful mood
      That over my spirit steals ;
Beneath their spell, and in verses rude,
      Whatever he dreams or feels ;

Whatever the fancies this Christmas Eve
      Are haunting the lonely man ;
Whether they gladden, or whether they grieve,
      He'll sing them as best he can,

Though some of the strings of his lyre are broke
      This holiest night of the year,
Who knows how its melody may wake
      A Christmas smile or a tear.

So on with the mystic song.
      With its meaning manifold—
      Two tones in every word,
      Two thoughts in every tone ;
In the measured words that move along
      One meaning shall be heard,
      One thought to all be told—
      But under it all, to me alone—
And under it all, to all unknown —
      As safe as under a coffin-lid,
      Deep meanings shall be hid—
      Find them out who can !
The thoughts concealed and unrevealed
      In the song of the lonely man.

*   *   *   *   *   *   *   *

I'm sitting alone in my silent room
This long December night,
Watching the fire-flame fill the gloom
With many a picture bright.
Ah ! how the fire can paint !
Its magic skill how strange !
How every spark
On the canvas dark
Draws figures and forms so quaint !
And how the pictures change !
One moment how they smile
And in less than a little while,
In the twinkling of an eye,
Like the gleam of a Summer sky,
The beaming smiles all die.

From gay to grave—from grave to gay,
The faces change in the shadows grey,
And just as I wonder who are they,
Over them all
Like a funeral pall,
The folds of the shadows droop and fall,
And the charm is gone
And every one
Of the pictures fade away.

Ah ! the fire within my grate
Hath more than Raphael's power,
Is more than Raphael's peer—
It paints for me in a little hour
More than he in a year ;
And the pictures hanging 'round me here
This holy Christmas eve

No Artist's pencil could create
No Painter's art conceive.
 Ah! those cheerful faces
 Wearing youthful graces;
I gaze on them until I seem
Half awake and half in dream.
 There are brows without a mark,
  Features bright without a shade;
  There are eyes without a tear;
 There are lips unused to sigh.
 Ah! never mind—you soon shall die!
  All those faces soon shall fade,
  Fade into the dreary dark,
  Like their pictures hanging here.
  ————Lo! those tearful faces,
  Bearing Age's traces!

I gaze on them, and they on me,
 Until I feel a sorrow steal
Through my heart so drearily;
 There are faces furrowed deep;
 There are eyes that used to weep;
  There are brows beneath a cloud;
 There are hearts that want to sleep.
 Never mind! the shadows creep
  From the Death-land; and a shroud,
 Tenderly as mother's arm,
 Soon shall shield the old from harm;
  Soon shall wrap its robe of Rest
  Round each sorrow-haunted breast.

—Ah! that face of Mother's,
 Sisters's, too, and Brother's —

And so many others,
Dear is every name—
And Ethel ! Thou art there—
With thy child-face sweet and fair,
    And thy heart so bright
    In its shroud so white ;—
    Just as I saw you last
    In the golden, happy past,
And you seem to wear
Upon your hair,
Your waving, golden hair,
    The smile of the setting sun—
    Ah ! me ! how years will run—
    But all the years cannot efface
    Your purest name, your sweetest grace
    From the heart that still is true
    Of all the world to you;
    The other faces shine
    But none so fair as thine,
And, wherever they are to-night, I know
    They look the very same
        As in their pictures hanging here
        This night, to Memory dear,
        And painted by the flames,
With tombstones in the background,
    And shadows for their frames.

    And thus, with my pictures only,
        And the fancies they unweave
    Alone, and yet not lonely,
        I keep my Christmas Eve.

I'm sitting alone in my pictured room—
    But, no ! they have vanished all—

I'm watching the fire-glow fade into gloom,
 I'm watching the ashes fall.
And far away back of the cheerful blaze
The beautiful visions of by-gone days
Are rising before my raptured gaze.

  Ah ! Christmas fire, so bright and warm,
  Hast thou a wizard's magic charm
To bring those far-off scenes so near
And make my past days meet me here ?
  Tell me—tell me—how is it ?
  The past is past, and here I sit,
  And there, lo ! there before me rise,
   Beyond yon glowing flame,
   The summer suns of childhood's skies,
    Yes—yes—the very same !
   I saw them rise long, long ago ;
   I played beneath their golden glow ;
    And I remember yet,
    l often cried with strange regret
    When in the West I saw them set.
   And there they are again ;
   The suns, the skies, the very days
   Of childhood, just beyond that blaze !
    But, ah ! such visions almost craze
    The old man's puzzled brain !
   I thought the Past was past !
    But, no, it cannot be ;
    'Tis here to-night with me !

   How is it, then ? the Past of Men
    Is part of one Eternity—
   The days of yore we so deplore,
   They are not dead—they are not fled,

They live and live for evermore.
And thus my Past comes back to me
With all its visions fair.

O, Past! could I go back to thee,
And live forever there!
But, no, there's frost upon my hair;
My feet have trod a path of Care;
And worn and wearied here I sit,
I am too tired to go to it.

And thus with visions only,
And the fancies they unweave,
Alone, and yet not lonely,
I keep my Christmas Eve.

I am sitting alone in my fire-lit room;
But, no! the fire is dying,
And the weary-voiced winds, in the outer gloom,
Are sad, and I hear them sighing.
The wind hath a voice to pine—
Plaintive, and pensive, and low,—
Hath it a heart, like mine or thine?
Knoweth it weal or woe?
How it wails, in a ghost-like strain,
Just against that window-pane!
As if it were tired of its long, cold flight,
And wanted to rest with me to-night:
Cease, night-winds, cease;
Why should you be sad?
This is a night of joy and peace,
And Heaven and Earth are glad!
But still the wind's voice grieves!
Perchance o'er the fallen leaves,

Which, in their Summer bloom,
Danced to the music of bird and breeze,
But, torn from the arms of their parent trees,
 Lie now in their wintry tomb,
 Mute types of man's own doom.

  And thus with the night winds only,
   And the fancies they unweave,
  Alone, and yet not lonely,
   I keep my Christmas Eve.

How long have I been dreaming here?
 Or have I dreamed at all?
My fire is dead—my pictures fled—
There's nothing left but shadows drear.
 Shadows on the wall:
 Shifting, flitting,   ·
 Round me sitting
 In my old arm chair—
  Rising—sinking
  Round me, thinking,
 Till, in the maze of many a dream,
 I'm not myself ; and I almost seem
 Like one of the shadows there.
  Well, let the shadows stay!
  I wonder who are they?
 I cannot say; but I almost believe
 They know to-night is Christmas Eve,
  And to-morrow Christmas Day.

Ah! there's nothing like a Christmas Eve!
 To change Life's bitter gall to sweet,
And change the sweet to gall again ;
 To take the thorns from out our feet—

The thorns and all their dreary pain,
Only to put them back again.

To take old stings from out our heart,
Old stings that made them bleed and smart,
Only to sharpen them the more,
And press them back to the heart's own core.

Ah! no eve is like the Christmas Eve!
Fears and hopes, and hopes and fears,
Tears and smiles, and smiles and tears,
Cheers and sighs, and sighs and cheers,
Sweet and bitter, bitter, sweet,
    Bright and dark, and dark and bright.
All these mingle, all these meet,
    In this great and solemn night.

Ah! there's nothing like a Christmas Eve!
To melt with kindly glowing heat,
From off our souls the snow and sleet,
The dreary drift of wintry years,
    Only to make the cold winds blow,
    Only to make a colder snow;
And make it drift, and drift, and drift,
In flakes so icy-cold and swift;
    Until the heart that lies below
    Is cold and colder than the snow.

    And thus with the shadows only,
        And the dreamings they unweave,
    Alone, and yet not lonely,
        I keep my Christmas Eve.

    'Tis passing fast!
My fireless, lampless room

Is a mass of moveless gloom ;
And without—a darkness vast,
 Solemn—starless—still !
 Heaven and Earth doth fill.
But list ! there soundeth a bell,
With a mystical ding, dong, dell !
 Is it, say, is it a funeral knell?
 Solemn and slow,
 Now loud—now low ;
Pealing the notes of human woe
Over the graves lying under the snow !
 Ah ! that pitiless ding, dong, dell !
 Trembling along the gale,
Under the stars and over the snow.
Why is it ? whence is it sounding so ?
 Is it the toll of a burial bell ?
 Or is it a spirit's wail ?
  Solemnly, mournfully
  Sad—and how lornfully !
   Ding, dong, dell !
  Whence is it ? who can tell ?
And the marvelous notes they sink and swell,
Sadder, and sadder, and sadder still !
How the sounds tremble ! how they thrill !
  Every tone
  So like a moan ;
As if the strange bell's stranger clang
Throbbed with a terrible human pang.
  Ding, dong, dell !
  Dismally—drearily—
  Ever so wearily.
 Far off and faint as a Requiem plaint
Floats the deep-toned voice of the mystic bell ;

Piercingly—thrillingly,
Icily—chillingly,
Near—and more near,
Drear, and more drear,
Soundeth the wild, wierd, ding, dong, dell!
Now sinking lower,
It tolleth slower!
I list, and I hear its sound no more.
And now, methinks, I know that bell,
Know it well—know its knell—
For I often heard it sound before.
It is a bell—yet not a bell
Whose sound may reach the ear!
It tolls a knell—yet not a knell
Which earthly sense may hear.
In every soul a bell of dole
Hangs ready to be tolled ;
And from that bell a funeral knell
Is often, outward rolled ;
And Memory is the Sexton grey
Who tolls the dreary knell
And nights like this he loves to sway
And swing his mystic bell.
'Twas that I heard and nothing more,
This lonely Christmas Eve ;
Then, for the dead I'll meet no more.
At Christmas let me grieve.

Night, be a Priest ! put your star-Stole on
And murmur a holy prayer
Over each grave, and for every one
Lying down lifeless there !
And over the dead stands the high priest Night,
Robed in his shadowy Stole ;

And beside him I kneel, as his Acolyte,
>> To respond to his prayer of dole.
>>> And list! he begins
>>> That psalm for sins,
The first of the mournful seven,
>>> Plaintive and soft
>>> It rises aloft,
Begging the mercy of Heaven
>>> To pity and forgive,
>>> For the sake of those who live.
The dead who have died unshriven.
>>> Miserere! Miserere!
Still your heart and hush your breath!
The voices of Despair and Death
>> Are shuddering through the psalm!
>>> Miserere! Miserere!
Lift your hearts! the terror dies!
Up in yonder sinless skies
>> The psalms sound sweet and calm!
>>> Miserere! Miserere!
Very low, in tender tones,
The music pleads, the music moans,
>> "I forgive, and have forgiven,
>>> The dead, whose hearts were shriven."

>> De profundis! De profundis!
Psalm of the dead and disconsolate!
Thou hast sounded through a thousand years,
And pealed above ten thousand biers;
And still, sad psalm, you mourn the fate
>>> Of sinners and of just,
When their souls are going up to God,
>>> Their bodies down to dust.

Dread hymn! you wring the saddest tears
    From mortal eyes that fall,
And your notes evoke the darkest fears
    That human hearts appall !
You sound o'er the good, you sound o'er the bad.
And ever your music is sad, so sad,
We seem to hear murmured, in every tone,
For the saintly, a blessing ; for sinners, a curse.
Psalm, sad Psalm ! you must pray and grieve
Over our Dead on this Christmas Eve.
      De profundis! De profundis !
And the Night chaunts the Psalm o'er the mortal ʳlay,
And the spirits immortal from far away,
To the music of Hope sing this sweet-toned lay :

You think of the Dead on Christmas eve,
    Wherever the Dead are sleeping ;
And we, from a Land where we may not grieve,
    Look tenderly down on your weeping.
You think us far ; we are very near,
    From you and the Earth though parted.
We sing to-night to console and cheer
    The hearts of the broken-hearted.
The earth watches over the lifeless clay
    Of each of its countless sleepers ;
And the sleepless Spirits that passed away
    Watch over all Earth's weepers.
We shall meet again in a brighter land,
    Where farewell is never spoken ;
We shall clasp each other hand in hand,
    And the clasp shall not be broken.
We shall meet again, in a bright, calm clime,
    Where we'll never know a sadness ;
And our lives shall be filled, like a Christmas chime,

With rapture and with gladness.
The snows shall pass from our graves away,
And you from the Earth, remember;
And the flowers of a bright, eternal May,
Shall follow Earth's December.
When you think of us, think not of the tomb
Where you laid us down in sorrow ;
But look aloft, and beyond Earth's gloom,
And wait for the great To-morrow.

And the Pontiff, Night, with his star-Stole on,
Whispereth soft and low :
Requiescat ! Requiescat !
Peace ! Peace ! to every one
For whom we grieve this Christmas Eve,
In their graves beneath the snow.

The stars in the far off Heaven
Have long since struck eleven !
And hark ! from Temple and from Tower,
Soundeth Time's grandest midnight hour,
Blessed by the Saviour's birth.
And Night putteth off the sable Stole,
Symbol of sorrow and sign of dole,
For one with many a starry gem,
To honor the Babe of Bethlehem,
Who comes to men, the King of them,
Yet comes without robe or diadem,
And all turn towards the holy East,
To hear the song of the Christmas Feast.

Four thousand years Earth waited,
Four thousand years men prayed,
Four thousand years the Nations sighed
That their King so long delayed.

The Prophets told His coming,
    The saintly for Him sighed;
And the star of the Babe of Bethlehem
    Shone o'er them when they died.

Their faces towards the Future—
    They longed to hail the Light
That in the after centuries,
    Would rise on Christmas night.

But still the Saviour tarried,
    Within His Father's home;
And the Nations wept and wondered why
    The Promised had not come.

At last Earth's hope was granted,
    And God was a Child of Earth;
And a thousand Angels chaunted
    The lowly midnight birth.

Ah! Bethlehem was grander
    That hour than Paradise;
And the light of Earth that night eclipsed
    The splendors of the skies.

Then let us sing the Anthem
    The Angels once did sing;
Until the music of love and praise,
    O'er whole wide world will ring.

    Gloria in excelsis!
      Sound the thrilling song!
    In excelsis Deo!
      Roll the Hymn along.

Gloria in excelsis!
  Let the Heavens ring;
In excelsis Deo!
  Welcome, new-born King.
Gloria in excelsis!
  Over the sea and land;
In excelsis Deo!
  Chaunt the Anthem grand.
Gloria in excelsis!
· Let us all rejoice;
In excelsis Deo!
  Lift each heart and voice.
Gloria in excelsis!
  Swell the Hymn on high;
In excelsis Deo!
  Sound it to the sky.
Gloria in excelsis!
  Sing it, sinful Earth!
In excelsis Deo!
  For the Saviour's birth.

Thus joyful and victoriously,
Glad and ever so gloriously;
High as the Heavens—wide as the Earth,
Swelleth the Hymn of the Saviour's birth.

  Lo! the Day is waking
    In the East afar;
  Dawn is faintly breaking—
    Sunk in every star.

  Christmas Eve has vanished
    With its shadows grey;
  All its griefs are banished
    By bright Christmas Day.

Joyful chimes are ringing
   O'er the land and seas,
And there comes glad singing,
   Borne on every breeze.

Little ones so merry
   Bed-clothes coyly lift,
And, in such a hurry,
   Prattle, " Christmas gift !"

Little heads so curly,
   Knowing Christmas laws.
Peep out very early
   For old "Santa Claus."

Little eyes are laughing
   O'er their Christmas toys,
Older ones are quaffing
   Cups of Christmas joys.

Hearts are joyous, cheerful,
   Faces all are gay ;
None are sad and tearful
   On bright Christmas Day.

Hearts are light and bounding,
   All from care are free ;
Homes are all resounding,
   With the sounds of glee.

Feet with feet are meeting,
   Bent on pleasure's way ;
Souls to souls give greeting
   Warm on Christmas Day.

Gifts are kept a-going
   Fast from hand to hand;
Blessings are a-flowing
   Over every land.

One vast wave of gladness
   Sweeps its world-wide way,
Drowning every sadness
   On this Christmas Day.

Merry, merry Christmas,
   Haste around the Earth ;
Merry, merry Christmas
   Scatter smiles and mirth.

Merry, merry Christmas,
   Be to one and all ;
Merry, merry Christmas
   Enter hut and hall.

Merry, merry Christmas,
   Be to rich and poor !
Merry, merry Christmas
   Stop at every door.

Merry, merry Christmas,
   Fill each heart with joy ;
Merry, merry Christmas
   To each girl and boy.

Merry, merry Christmas,
   Better gifts than gold ;
Merry, merry Christmas
   To the young and old.

Merry, merry Christmas !
   May the coming year
Bring as merry a Christmas
   And as bright a cheer.

"FAR AWAY."

FAR AWAY! what does it mean?
A change of heart with a change of place?
When footsteps pass from scene to scene,
Fades soul from soul with face from face?
Are hearts the slaves or lords of space?

"Far Away!" what does it mean?
Does distance sever There from Here?
Can leagues of land part hearts?—I ween
They cannot;—for the trickling tear
Says "Far Away," means, "Far More Near."

"Far away!"—the mournful miles
Are but the mystery of space
That blends our sighs, but parts our smiles,
For love will find a meeting place
When face is farthest off from face.

"Far away!" we meet in dreams,
As 'round the Altar of the Night
Far parted stars send down their gleams
To meet in one embrace of light,
And make the brow of darkness bright.

"Far away!" we meet in tears,
That tell the path of weary feet
And all the Good-byes of the years
But make the wanderer's welcome sweet.
The rains of parted clouds thus meet.—

" Far away ! " we meet in prayer,
   You know the temple and the shrine ;
  Before it bows the brow of care,
    Upon it tapers dimly shine ;
    'Tis Mercy's Home, and yours and mine.—

" Far away ! " it falls between
  What is to-day, and what has been ;
  But ah ! what is meets what is not,
  In every hour and every spot,
  Where lips breathe on " I have forgot."

" Far away ! " there is no Far !
  Nor days nor distance e'er can bar
  My spirit from your spirits ; —nay,
  Farewell may waft a face away,
  But still with you my heart will stay.

" Far away ! " I sing its song,
  But while the music moves along,
  From out each word an echo clear
  Falls trembling on my spirit's ear,
" Far away " means Far more near.

LISTEN.

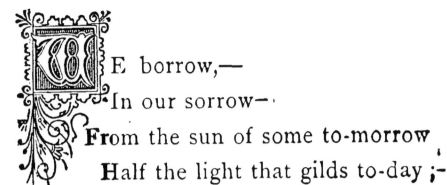

WE borrow,—
In our sorrow—
From the sun of some to-morrow
Half the light that gilds to-day ;-

And the splendor,
Flashes tender,—
O'er Hope's footsteps, to defend her
From the fears that haunt the way.

We never,—
Here can sever—
Any Now from the Forever
Interclasping Near and Far !
For each minute
Holds within it
All the hours of the Infinite.
As one sky holds every star.

WRECKED.

HE winds are singing a death-knell
   Out on the main to-night ;
The sky droops low,—and many a bark,
   That sailed from harbors bright,
     Like many an one before
     Shall enter port no more :
And a wreck shall drift to some unknown shore,
   Before to-morrow's light.

The clouds are hanging a death-pall
   Over the sea to-night,
The stars are veiled—and the hearts that sailed
   Away from harbors bright,
Shall sob their last for their quiet home—
And sobbing, sink 'neath the whirling foam
   Before the morning's light.

The waves are weaving a death-shroud
   Out on the main to-night ;
Alas ! the last prayer whispered there
   By lips with terror white
     Over the ridge of gloom
     Not a star will loom !
God help the souls that will meet their doom
   Before the dawn of light.

The breeze is singing a Joy song
    Over the sea to-day ;
The storm is dead,—and the waves are red
    With the flush of the morning's ray ;—
And the sleepers sleep, but beyond the deep,
The eyes that watch for the ships, shall weep
    For the hearts they bore away.

SORROW AND THE FLOWERS.

A MEMORIAL WREATH TO C. F.

SORROW :

GARLAND for a grave ! Fair flowers that bloom,
    And only bloom to fade as fast away,
We twine your leaflets 'round our Claudia's tomb,
    And with your dying beauty crown her clay.

Ye are the tender types of life's decay ;
    Your beauty, and your love-enfragranced breath,
From out the hand of June, or heart of May,
    Fair flowers ! tell less of life and more of death.

My name is Sorrow. I have knelt at graves,
    All o'er the weary world, for weary years ;
I kneel there still, and still my anguish laves
    The sleeping dust with moaning streams of tears.

And yet, the while I garland graves as now,
    I bring fair wreaths to deck the place of woe,
Whilst Joy is crowning many a living brow,
    I crown the poor frail dust that sleeps below.

She was a Flower—fresh, fair and pure and frail ;
    A Lily in life's morning : God is sweet ;
He reached His hand, there rose a mother's wail ;
    Her Lily drooped : 'tis blooming at His feet.

Where are the flowers to crown the faded Flower ?
    I want a garland for another grave ;
And who will bring them from the dell and bower ?
    To crown what God hath taken, with what Heav‹
      en gave.

As though ye heard my voice, ye heed my will ;
    Ye come with fairest flowers : give them to me,
To crown our Claudia. Love leads Memory still,
    To prove at graves Love's immortality.

WHITE ROSE :

Her grave is not a grave ; it is a Shrine,
    Where innocence reposes,
Bright over which God's stars must love to shine,
    And where, when Winter closes,
Fair Spring shall come, and in her garland twine,
Just like this hand of mine,
    The whitest of white roses.

LAUREL :

I found it on a mountain slope,
    The sunlight on its face ;
It caught from clouds a smile of hope
    That brightened all the place.

They wreathe with it the warrior's brow,
 And crown the chieftain's head ;
But the Laurel's leaves love best to grace
 The garland of the dead.

WILD FLOWER :

I would not live in a garden,
 But far from the haunts of men ;
Nature herself was my warden ;
 I lived in a lone little glen.
A Wild Flower out of the wildwood.
 Too wild for even a name ;
As strange and as simple as childhood.
 And wayward, yet sweet all the same.

WILLOW BRANCH :

To Sorrow's own sweet crown,
 With simple grace,
The Weeping-Willow bends her branches down
 Just like a mother's arm,
 To shield from harm,
The dead within their resting place.

LILY :

The Angel Flower of all the flowers ;
 Its sister flowers,
 In all the bowers,
Worship the Lily, for it brings,
 Wherever it blooms,
 On shrines or tombs,
A dream surpassing earthly sense
Of Heaven's own stainless innocence.

VIOLET LEAVES :

It is too late for Violets,
 I only bring their leaves ;
I looked in vain for Mignonettes
 To grace the crown grief weaves ;
For queenly May, upon her way,
  Robs half the bowers
   Of all their flowers,
 And leaves but leaves to June,
 Ah ! beauty fades so soon ;
And the valley grows lonely in spite of the sun,
For flowrets are fading fast, one by one.
  Leaves for a grave, leaves for a garland,
  Leaves for a Little Flower, gone to the Far Land.

FORGET-ME-NOT:

" Forget me not." The sad words strangely quiver,
On lips like shadows falling on a river,
  Flowing away,
  By night, by day,
  Flowing away forever.
The mountain whence the river springs,
 Murmurs to it, " Forget me not ;"
The little stream runs on and sings
 On to the sea, and every spot
  It passes by
  Breathes forth a sigh,
 " Forget me not," " Forget me not."

A GARLAND :

I bring this for her mother ; ah ! who knows
The lonely deeps within a mother's heart ?
Beneath the wildest wave of woe that flows
Above, around her, when her children part,

There is a sorrow, silent, dark, and lone;
It sheds no tears, it never maketh moan.

Whene'er a child dies from a mother's arms,
A grave is dug within the mother's heart :
She watches it alone ; no words of art
Can tell the story of her vigils there.
This garland fading even while 'tis fair,
It is a mother's memory of a grave,
When God hath taken her whom Heaven gave.

SORROW :

Farewell ! I go to crown the dead ;
Yet ye have crowned yourselves to-day,
For they, whose hearts so faithful, love
The lonely grave—the very clay ;
They crown themselves with richer gems
Than flash in royal diadems.

A THOUGHT.

HEARTS that are great beat never loud,
    They muffle their music, when they come ;
They hurry away from the thronging crowd
    With bended brows and lips half dumb.

And the world looks on and mutters—" Proud."
    But when great hearts have passed away
Men gather in awe and kiss their shroud,
    And in love they kneel around their clay.

Hearts that are great are always lone,—
    They never will manifest their best ;—
Their greatest greatness is unknown,—
    Earth knows a little ~ God, the rest.

"DREAMING."

HE moan of a Wintry soul
   Melted into a Summer-song,
And the words, like the wavelet's roll
   Moved murmuringly along.

And the Song flowed far and away
   Like the Voice of a half-sleeping rill —
Each wave of it lit by a ray,—
   But the sound was so soft and so still,—

And the tone was so gentle and low,—
   None heard the song till it had passed ;—
Till the echo, that followed its now
   Came dreamingly back from the Past.

'Twas too late !—a song never returns
   That passes our pathway,—unheard ; —
As dust lying dreaming in Urns
   Is the Song lying dead in a word.

For the birds of the skies have a nest —
   And the winds have a home where they sleep·
And songs, like our souls, need a rest,
   Where they murmur the while we may weep.

*   ·:   *   *   ·:   ·:   ·:   *

But songs—like the birds o'er the foam,
   Where the storm-wind is beating their breast
Fly shoreward—and oft find a home
   In the shelter of words where they rest.

"YESTERDAYS."

GONE ! and they return no more,
    But they leave a light in the heart,
The murmur of waves that kiss a shore
    Will never, I know, depart.

Gone ! yet with us still they stay,
    And their memories throb thro' life,
The music that hushes or stirs to-day,
    Is toned by their calm or strife.

Gone ! and yet they never go !
    We kneel at the shrine of Time,
'Tis a mystery no man may know,
    Nor tell in a Poet's rhyme.

"TO-DAYS!"

BRIEF while they last,
　　Long when they are gone;
They catch from the past,
　　A light to still live on.

Brief! yet I ween,
　　A day may be an age,
The Poet's pen may screen
　　Heart-stories on one page.

Brief! but in them,
　　From eve back to morn,
Some find the gem,
　　Many find the thorn.

Brief! minutes pass!
　　Soft as flakes of snow,
Shadows o'er the grass
　　Could not swifter go.

Brief! but along
　　All the after-years
To-day will be a song
　　Of smiles or of tears.

"TO-MORROWS!"

OD knows all things,—but we
　　In darkness walk our ways.
We wonder what will be,
　　We ask the Nights and Days.

Their lips are sealed ; at times
　　The Bards, like Prophets see,
And rays rush o'er their rhymes
　　From suns of " days to be."

They see To-morrow's Heart,
　　They read To-morrow's face,
They grasp,—is it by art?
　　The far To-morrow's trace.

They see what is unseen,
　　And hear what is unheard—
And To-morrow's shade or sheen
　　Rests on the Poet's word.

As Seers see a star
　　Beyond the brow of Night :
So Poets scan the Far,
　　Prophetic when they write.

They read a human face,
　　As Readers read their Page,
The while their thought will trace
　　A life from youth to Age.

They have a mournful Gift,
   Their verses, oft, are tears;
And sleepless eyes they lift
   To look adown the years.

To-morrows are To-days!
   Is it not more than art?
When all life's winding ways
   Meet in the Poet's Heart.

The Present meets the Past,
   The Future, too, is there;
The First enclasps the Last,
   And Never folds Fore'er.

It is not all a dream;
   A Poet's thought is Truth;
The things that are—and seem
   From Age far back to Youth—

He holds the tangled threads;
   His hands unravel them;
He knows the Hearts and Heads
   For Thorns, or Diadem.

Ask him, and he will see,
   What your To-morrows are;
He'll sing "What is to be"
   Beneath each sun and star.

To-morrows! Dread Unknown!
   What fates may they not bring?
What is the chord, the tone?
   The key in which they sing?

I see a thousand throngs,
  To-morrows for them wait ;
I hear a thousand songs
  Intoning each one's fate.

And yours ?   What will it be ?
  Hush song ! and let me pray !
God sees it all, I see
  A long, lone, winding way ;

And more ! no matter what !
  Crosses and crowns you wear :
My song may be forgot,
  But Thou shalt not, in Prayer.

"INEVITABLE."

WHAT has been will be,—
  'Tis the under-law of life,—
'Tis the song of sky and sea,—
  To the Key of calm and strife.—

For guard we as we may,
  What is to be will be,
The dark must fold each day—
  The shore must gird each sea.

All things are ruled by law,—
  'Tis only in man's will
You meet a feeble flaw,—
  But fate is weaving still—

The web and woof of life
  With hands that have no hearts—
Thro' calmness and thro' strife
  Despite all human arts.

For fate is master here—
  He laughs at human wiles,—
He sceptres every tear,
  And fetters any smile.

What is to be will be—
  We cannot help ourselves,
The waves ask not the sea
  Where lies the shore that shelves.

The law is coldest steel
  We live beneath its sway—
It cares not what we feel,
  And so pass night and day.

And sometimes we may think
  This cannot,—will not be—
Some waves must rise,—some sink
  Out on the midnight sea.

And we are weak as waves
  That sink upon the shore,
We go down into Graves—
  Fate chaunts the Nevermore ;

*   *   *   *   *   *

Cometh a Voice ! Kneel down !
  'Tis God's,—there is no Fate—
He giveth the Cross and Crown,
  He opens the jeweled gate—

He watcheth with such eyes
   As only mothers own,—
" Sweet Father in the skies!
   Ye call us to a Throne."

There is no Fate,—God's love
   Is law beneath each law,
And law all laws above
   Fore'er,—without a flaw.—

HOPE!

HINE eyes are dim :
   A mist hath gathered there :
Around their rim,
   Float many clouds of care,
   And there is sorrow every—every where.

   But there is God,
      Every—everywhere ;
   Beneath His rod,
      Kneel thou, adown in prayer.

For Grief is God's own kiss,
   Upon a soul.
Look up ! the sun of bliss
   Will shine where storm-clouds roll.

Yes, weeper! weep!
 'Twill not be evermore;
I know the darkest deep
 Hath e'en the brightest shore.

So tired! so tired!
 A cry of half despair;
Look! at your side—
 And see who standeth there!

Your Father! Hush,
 A Heart beats in His breast—
Now rise and rush
 Into His Arms—and rest.

"FAREWELLS!"

HEY are so sad to say: no poem tells
The agony of hearts that dwells
In lone and last Farewells.

They are like deaths: they bring a wintry chill
To summer's roses, and to summer's rill;
And yet we breathe them still.

For pure as altar-lights hearts pass away;
Hearts! we said to them, "Stay with us! stay!
And they said, sighing as they said it, "Nay."

The sunniest days are shortest ; darkness tells
The starless story of the Night that dwells
In lone and last Farewells.

Two faces meet here, there, or anywhere :
Each wears the thoughts the other face may wear ;
Their hearts may break, breathing, " Farewell fore'er."

SONG OF THE RIVER.

RIVER went singing, adown to the sea,
    A-singing—low—singing—
And the dim rippling river said softly to me
    " I'm bringing,—a-bringing—
      While floating along—
      A beautiful song
To the shores that are white where the waves are so
    weary,
To the beach that is burdened with wrecks that are
    dreary.
      A song sweet and calm
      As the peacefulest psalm ;
      And the shore that was sad
      Will be grateful and glad,—
And the weariest wave from its dreariest dream
Will wake to the sound of the song of the stream :
      And the tempests shall cease
      And there shall be Peace."

From the fairest of fountains
And farthest of mountains,
From the stillness of snow
Came the stream in its flow.

Down the slopes where the rocks are gray,
Thro' the vales where the flowers are fair—
Where the sunlight flashed—where the shadows lay
Like stories that cloud a face of care,—
The river ran on,—and on,—and on
Day and night, and night and day
Going and going ; and never gone,
Longing to flow to the " Far away "—
Staying and staying, and never still
Going and staying as if one will,
Said " Beautiful River go to the sea,"
And another will whispered, "Stay with me :"
And the river made answer, soft and low—
" I go and stay "—" I stay and go."

But what is the song, I said, at last
To the passing river that never passed ;—
And a white, white wave whispered, " List to me,
I'm a note in the song for the beautiful sea,
A song whose grand accents no earth-din may sever
And the river flows on in the same mystic key
That blends in one chord the ' Forever and Never.' "

DECEMBER 15th, 1878.

DREAMLAND.

OVER the silent sea of sleep,
Far away ! far away !
Over a strange and starlit deep,
Where the beautiful shadows sway,-
Dim, in the dark—
Glideth a bark—
Where never the waves of a tempest roll-
Bearing the very "soul of the soul"
Alone, all alone—
Far away—far away,
To shores all-unknown
In the wakings of the day ;—
To the lovely land of dreams,
Where what is meets with what seems
Brightly-dim ;—dimly-bright
Where the suns meet stars at night,
Where the darkness meets the light
Heart to heart, face to face
In an infinite embrace.

❖   ❖   ❖   ❖   ❖

Mornings break,
And we wake,
And we wonder where we went
In the bark
Thro' the dark.
But our wonder is mis-spent
For no Day can cast a light
On the dreamings of the Night.

LINES.

SOMETIMES from the Far-away,—
    Wing a little thought to me ;—
In the night, or in the day
    It will give a rest to me,

I have praise of many here,—
    And the world gives me renown ;
Let it go—give me one tear
    'Twill be a jewel in my crown.

What care I for earthly fame?
    How I shrink from all its glare !—
I would rather that my name
    Would be shrined in some one's prayer.

Many hearts are all too much ;—
    Or too little in their praise ;—
I would rather feel the touch
    Of one prayer that thrills all days.

A SONG.

PURE faced Page! waiting so long
    To welcome my Muse and me;—
Fold to thy breast, like a mother, the song
    That floats from my spirit to thee.

And Song! sound soft as the streamlet sings
    And sweet as the Summer's birds,
And pure and bright and white be the wings
    That will waft thee into words.

Yea! fly as the sea-birds fly over the sea
    To rest on the far off beach,—
And breathe forth the message I trust to thee,
    Tear-toned on the shores of speech.

But ere you go, dip your snowy wing
    In a wave of my spirit's deep,—
In the wave that is purest,—then haste and bring
    A song to the hearts that weep.

Oh! bring it,—and sing it,—its notes are tears;
    Its octaves, the octaves of grief;
Who knows but its tones in the far off years
    May bring to the lone heart relief.

Yea! bring it,—and sing it,—a worded moan
    That sweeps thro' the minors of woe,—
With mystical meanings in every tone,
    And sounds like the sea's lone flow.

* * * * * * * *

And the thoughts take the wings of words and float
   Out of my spirit to thee,—
But the song dies away into only one note
   And sounds but in only one key.

And the Note !—'tis the wail of the weariest wave
   That sobs on the lonliest shore,—
And the Key ! never mind ! it comes out of a grave !
   And the Chord !—'tis a sad " Nevermore."

And just like the wavelet that moans on the beach
   And sighing, sinks back to the sea,—
So my song—it just touches the rude shores of speech,
   And its music melts back into me.

Yea ! song ! shrink back to my spirit's lone deep,
   Let others hear only thy moan,—
But I—I forever shall hear the grand sweep
   Of thy mighty and tear-burdened tone.

Sweep on ! mighty song—sound down in my heart
   As a storm sounding under a sea ;—
Not a sound of thy music shall pass into art,
   Nor a note of it float out from me.

PARTING.

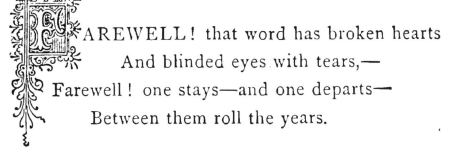

FAREWELL! that word has broken hearts
  And blinded eyes with tears,—
Farewell! one stays—and one departs—
  Between them roll the years.

No wonder why who say it think—
  Farewell! he may fare ill;
No wonder that their spirits sink
  And all their hopes grow chill.

Good-bye! that word makes faces pale
  And fills the soul with fears;
Good-bye! two words that wing a wail
  Which flutters down the years.

No wonder they who say it, feel
  Such pangs for those who go—
Good-bye! they wish the parted weal,
  But ah! they may meet woe.

Adieu! such is the word for us,—
  'Tis more than word—'tis prayer,—
They do not part, who do part thus,
  For God is everywhere.

ST. STEPHEN.

IRST champion of the Crucified !
    Who when the fight began
Between the Church and worldly pride
So nobly fought—so nobly died—
    The foremost in the van ;—
While rallied to your valiant side
    The red-robed martyr-band ;—
To-night with glad and high acclaim
We venerate thy saintly name ;
Accept St. Stephen to thy praise
And glory—these our lowly lays.

The chosen twelve with chrismed hand
    And burning zeal within
Led forth their small yet fearless band
On Pentecost—and took their stand
    Against the world and sin—
While rang aloud the battle-cry
" The hated Christians—all must die,
    As died the Nazarine before,
The God they believe in and adore."

Yet Stephen's heart quailed not with fear
    At persecution's cry,
But loving as he did, the cause
Of Jesus—and His faith and laws
    Prepared himself to die—
He faced his foes with burning zeal,

Such zeal as only Saints can feel,
He told them how the Lord had stood
Within their midst, so great and good,
How He had through Judea trod,
How wonders marked His way—the God—
How He had cured the blind—the lame,
The deaf, the palsied and the maimed,—
And how with awful, wondrous might
He raised the dead to life and light,—
And how His people knew Him not,
Had eyes and still had seen Him not,
Had ears and still had heard Him not,
Had hearts and comprehended not.

Then said he pointing to the right
Where darkly rose Golgotha's hight—
" There have ye slain the holy One
Your Saviour and God's only Son."

They gnashed their teeth in raging ire,
    Those dark and cruel men,
They vowed a vengeance deep and dire
    Against Saint Stephen then.
Yet he was calm ;—a radiant light
    Around his forehead gleamed,
He raised his eyes—a wondrous sight
He saw—so grand it was and bright,—
His soul was filled with such delight
    That he an angel seemed.
Then spoke the Saint—" A vision grand
    Bursts on me from above,
The doors of heaven open stand,
And at the Father's own right hand
    I see the Lord I love"—

" Away with him "—the rabble cry,
   With swelling rage and hate,
But Stephen still gazed on the sky,
His heart was with his Lord on high,
   He heeded not his fate.—
The gathering crowd in fury wild
   Rush on the raptured Saint,
And seize their victim mute and mild,
Who like his Master though reviled
   Still uttered no complaint.

With angry shouts they rend the air ;
   They drag him to the city gate ;
They bind his hands and feet, and there,
While whispered he for them a prayer,
   The Marty meets his fate.

First fearless witness to his belief
   In Jesus Crucified,
The red-robed Martyrs' noble chief,
   Thus for his Master died.
And to the end of time his name
Our Holy Church shall e'er proclaim,
And with a mother's pride shall tell
How her great proto-Martyrs fell.

A FLOWER'S SONG.

STAR ! Star ! why dost thou shine
 Each night upon my brow ?
Why dost thou make me dream the dreams
 That I am dreaming now ?

Star ! Star ! thy home is high—
 I am of humble birth ;
Thy feet walk shining o'er the sky,
 Mine, only on the earth.

Star ! Star ! why make me dream ?
 My dreams are all untrue :
And why is Sorrow's Dark for me
 And Heaven's Bright for you ?

Star ! Star ! oh ! hide thy ray !
 And take it off my face ;
Within my lowly home I stay,—
 Thou,—in thy lofty place.

Star ! Star ! and still I dream,—
 Along thy light afar !
I seem to soar until I seem
 To be, like you, a star.

THE STAR'S SONG.

LOWER! Flower! why repine!
    God knows each creature's place;
He hides within me when I shine,—
    And your leaves hide his face.

And you are near as I to Him,
    And you reveal as much
Of that Eternal soundless hymn
    Man's words may never touch.

God sings to man through all my rays
    That wreathe the brow of night,
And walks with me thro' all my ways—
    The Everlasting Light.

Flower! Flower! why repine?
    He chose on lowly earth
And not in Heaven where I shine
    His Bethlehem and birth.

Flower! Flower! I see Him pass
    Each hour of night and day,
Down to an Altar and a Mass
    Go thou,—and fade away—

Fade away upon His shrine!
    Thy light is brighter far
Than all the light wherewith I shine
    In Heaven,—as a star.

DEATH OF THE FLOWER.

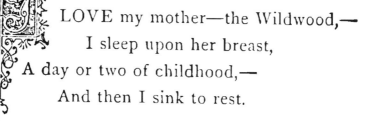

LOVE my mother—the Wildwood,—
    I sleep upon her breast,
A day or two of childhood,—
    And then I sink to rest.

I had once a lovely sister—
    She was cradled by my side.
But one summer-day I missed her,
    She had gone to deck a bride.

And I had another sister,
    With cheeks all bright with bloom ;
And another morn I missed her,
    She had gone to wreathe a tomb.

And they told me they had withered,
    On the bride's brow and the grave ;—
Half-an-hour,—and all their fragrance
    Died away,—which Heaven gave.

Two sweet-faced girls came walking
    . Thro' my lonely home one day,—
And I overheard them talking
    Of an Altar on their way.

They were culling flowers around me—
    And I said a little prayer
To go with them ;—and they found me,—
    And upon an Altar fair—

Where the Eucharist was lying
 On its mystical death-bed,
I felt myself a-dying,
 While the Mass was being said.

But I lived a little longer,
 And I prayed there all the day,
Till the Evening-Benediction,
 When my poor life passed away.

NOW.

SOMETIMES a single hour
 Rings thro' a long life-time,
As from a temple-tower
 There often falls a chime
From blessed bells,—that seems
To fold in Heaven's dreams
 Our spirits round a shrine;
 Hath such an hour been thine?

Sometimes,—who knoweth why?
 One minute holds a power
 That shadows eve'ry hour
Dialed in life's sky.
 A cloud that is a speck
When seen from far away
 May be a storm,—and wreck
The joys of every day.

Sometimes,—it seems not much,
   'Tis scarcely felt at all,—
Grace gives a gentle touch
   To hearts for once and all,—
Which in the spirit's strife
   May all unnoticed be.
And yet it rules a life :
   Hath this e'er come to thee ?

Sometimes one little word
   Whispered sweet and fleet,
That scarcely can be heard
   Our ears will sudden meet,
And all life's hours along
   That whisper may vibrate,
And like a wizard's song
   Decide our ev'ry fate.

Sometimes a sudden look,
   That falleth from some face,
Will steal into each nook
   Of life,—and leave its trace ;
To haunt us to the last,
   And sway our ev'ry will
Thro' all the days to be
   For goodness or for ill ;
Hath this e'er come to thee ?

Sometimes one minute folds
   The hearts of all the years,—
Just like the heart that holds
   The Infinite in tears ;
There be such things as this :
   Who knoweth why or how ?
A life of woe or bliss
   Hangs on some little Now.

SINGING-BIRD.

IN the valley of my life
　　Sings a " Singing-Bird,"
And its voice thro' calm and strife
　　Is sweetly heard.

In the day and thro' the night
　　Sound the notes,—
And its song thro' Dark and Bright
　　Ever floats.

Other warblers cease to sing
　　And their voices rest,—
And they fold their weary wing
　　In their quiet nest—

But my Singing-Bird still sings
　　Without a cease ;
And each song, it murmurs, brings
　　My spirit peace.

" Singing-Bird ! " oh ! " Singing-Bird ! "
　　No one knows,
When your holy songs are heard,
　　What repose

Fills my life and soothes my heart;
　　But I fear
The day—thy songs, if we must part,
　　I 'll never hear.

But " Singing-Bird ! " ah ! " Singing-Bird ! "
　　Should this e'er be,
The dreams of all thy songs I heard
　　Shall sing for me.

GOD IN THE NIGHT.

DEEP in the dark I hear the feet of God,—
He walks the world ;—He puts His holy hand
On ev'ry sleeper,—only puts his hand—
Within it benedictions for each one ;—
Then passes on,—but ah ! whene'er He meets
A watcher waiting for Him,—He is glad.
(Does God, like man, feel lonely in the dark ?)
He rests His hand upon the watcher's brow,—
But more than that,—He leaves His very breath
Upon the watcher's soul,—and more than this,
He stays for holy hours where watchers pray,—
And more than that—He oftimes lifts the veils
That hide the Visions of the world unseen.
The brightest sanctities of highest souls
Have blossomed into beauty in the dark.
How extremes meet ! the very darkest crimes,
That blight the souls of men, are strangely born
Beneath the shadows of the holy night.

Deep in the dark I hear His holy feet,—
Around Him rustle Archangelic wings;—
He lingers by the Temple where His Christ
Is watching in His Eucharistic sleep ;
And where poor hearts in sorrow cannot rest
He lingers there to soothe their weariness.
Where mothers weep above the dying child
He stays to bless the mothers' bitter tears,
And consecrates the cradle of her child,

Which is to her her spirit's awful cross.
He shudders past the haunts of sin,—yet leaves
E'er there a mercy for the wayward hearts.
Still as a shadow through the night he moves
With hands all full of blessings,—and with heart
All full of everlasting love ; ah me !
How God does love this poor and sinful world !

The stars behold Him as he passes on
And arch His path of mercy with their rays.
The stars are grateful,—He gave them their light,
And now they give Him back the light He gave.
The shadows tremble in adoring awe ;
They feel His Presence and they know His Face.
The shadows, too, are grateful,—could they pray,
How they would flower all His way with prayers !
The sleeping trees wake up from all their dreams,—
Were their leaves lips, ah me ! how they would sing
A grand Magnificat as His Mary sang.
The lowly grasses and the fair-faced flowers
Watch their Creator as he passes on
And mourn they have no hearts to love their God,
And sigh they have no souls to be beloved.
Man,—only man—the image of his God—
Lets God pass by when He walks forth at night.

HEN I am dead,—and all will soon forget
My words,—and face,—and ways;
I, somehow, think I'll walk beside thee yet
Adown thy after days.—

I die first,—and you will see my grave,—
But child! you must not cry;—
For my dead hand will brighest blessings wave
O'er you from yonder sky.—

You must not weep,—I believe I'd hear your tears
Tho' sleeping in a tomb,—
My rest would not be rest, if in your years
There floated clouds of gloom.—

For,—from the first,--your soul was dear to mine
And dearer it became,—
Until my soul, in every prayer would twine
Thy name;—my child! thy name.

You came to me in girlhood pure and fair,—
And in your soul—and face—
I saw a likeness to another there
In every trace and grace.

You came to me in girlhood—and you brought,—
An image back to me;—
No matter what,—or whose,—I often sought
Another's soul in thee.—

Didst ever mark how, sometimes, 1 became—
    Gentle though I be,—
Gentler than ever when I called thy name,
    Gentlest to thee?

You came to me in girlhood; as your guide,—
    1 watched your spirit's ways ;—
We walked God's holy valleys side by side,—
    And so went on the days.—

And so went on the years,—'tis five and more,—
    Your soul is fairer now ;—
A light as of a sunset on a shore
    Is falling on my brow,—

Is falling,—soon to fade,—when I am Dead
    Think this, my child ! of me ;—
I never said,—I never could have said
    Ungentle words to thee.—

I treated you,—as I would treat a flower,—
    1 watched you with such care ;—
And from my lips God heard in many an hour
    Your name in many a prayer.

I watched the flower's growth,—so fair it grew,—
    On not a leaf a stain ;
Your soul to purest thoughts so sweetly true ;
    I did not watch in vain.—

I guide you still,—in my steps still you tread ;—
    Towards God these ways are set ;—
T'will soon be over—child ! —when I am dead
    I'll watch—and guide you yet.

'Tis better far that I should go before,—
    And you awhile should stay ;—
But I will wait upon the golden shore
    To meet my child some day.—

When I am dead ; in some lone after time,
    If crosses come to thee,—
You'll think—remembering this simple rhyme—
    " He holds a crown for me."—

I guide you here,—I go before you there—
    But here or there,—I know
Whether the roses, or the thorny crown you wear
    I'll watch where'er you go,—

And wait until you come ;—when I am dead
    Think, sometimes, child ! of this ;
You must not weep—follow where I led,
    I wait for you in bliss.

REUNITED.

WRITTEN AFTER THE YELLOW FEVER EPIDEMIC OF 1878.

PURER than thy own white snow ;
    Nobler than thy mountains' height ;
Deeper than the ocean's flow ;
    Stronger than thy own proud might ;
Oh ! Northland, to thy sister land,
Was late, thy mercy's generous deed and grand.

REUNITED.

Nigh twice ten years, the sword was sheathed:
  Its mist of green, o'er battle plain,
For nigh two decades Spring had breathed:
  And yet the crimson life-blood stain,
From passive swards, had never paled;
Nor fields, where all were brave and some had failed.

Between the Northland—Bride of snow,
  And Southland—brightest sun's fair bride,
Swept, deepening ever, in its flow,
  The stormy wake, in war's dark tide:
No hand might clasp, across the tears
And blood and anguish of four deathless years.

When Summer, like a rose in bloom,
  Had blossomed from the bud of Spring;
Oh! who could deem, the dews of doom,
  Upon the blushing lips, could cling?
And who could believe, its fragrant light,
Would e'er be freighted, with the breath of blight.

Yet o'er the Southland, crept the spell,
  That e'en from out its brightness spread;
And prostrate, powerless, she fell;
  Rachel-like, amid her dead.
Her bravest, fairest, purest, best,
The waiting grave would welcome, as its guest.

The Northland, strong in love, and great,
  Forgot the stormy days of strife;
Forgot that souls, with dreams of hate,
  Or unforgiveness, e'er were rife.
Forgotten was each thought and hushed;
Save, she was generous and her foe was crushed.

No hand might clasp, from land to land—
   Yea—there was one to bridge the tide ;
For at the touch of Mercy's hand,
   The North and South stood side by side :
The Bride of Snow, the Bride of Sun,
In Charity's espousals, are made one.

" Thou givest back my sons again,"
   The Southland to the Northland cries ;
" For all my dead, on battle plain,
   Thou biddest my dying now uprise :
I still my sobs ; I cease my tears ;
And thou hast recompensed my anguished years.

" Blessings on thine every wave,
   Blessings on thine every shore,
Blessings that from sorrows save,
   Blessings giving more and more,
For all thou gavest thy sister land,
Oh ! Northland, in thy generous deed and grand."

C. S. A.

O we weep for the heroes who died for us?
Who living were true and tried for us,
  And dying sleep side by side for us ;—
      The Martyr-band
      That hallowed our land
With the blood they shed in a tide for us.

Ah! fearless on many a day for us
They stood in the front of the fray for us,
And held the foeman at bay for us,
  And tears should fall
  Fore'er o'er all
Who fell while wearing the gray for us.

How many a glorious name for us,
How many a story of fame for us,
They left,—would it not be a blame for us,
  If their memories part
  From our land and heart,
And a wrong to them, and shame for us?

No—no—no—they were brave for us,
And bright were the lives they gave for us,—
The land they struggled to save for us
  Will not forget
  Its warriors yet
Who sleep in so many a grave for us.

On many and many a plain for us
Their blood poured down all in vain for us,
Red, rich and pure,—like a rain for us;
  They bleed,—we weep,
  We live,—they sleep—
"All Lost"—the only refrain for us.

But their memories e'er shall remain for us,
And their names, bright names, without stain for us,-
The glory they won shall not wane for us,
  In legend and lay
  Our heroes in gray
Shall forever live over again for us.

THE SEEN AND THE UNSEEN.

NATURE is but the outward vestibule
Which God has placed before an unseen shrine;
The visible is but a fair, bright vale
That winds around the great Invisible;
The finite,—it is nothing but a smile
That flashes from the face of Infinite,—
A smile with shadows on it,—and 'tis sad
Men bask beneath the smile but oft forget
The loving Face that very smile conceals.
The changeable is but the broidered robe
Enwrapped about the great Unchangeable;
The audible is but an echo faint
Low whispered from the far Inaudible;
This earth is but an humble Acolyte
A-kneeling on the lowest Altar-step
Of this Creation's Temple, at the Mass
Of Supernature,—just to ring the bell
At Sanctus! Sanctus! Sanctus! while the world
Prepares its heart for Consecration's hour.

Nature is but the ever-rustling veil
Which God is wearing like the Carmelite
Who hides her face behind her virgin-veil
To keep it all unseen from mortal eyes,
Yet by her vigils and her holy prayers
And ceaseless sacrifices night and day
Shields souls from sin—and many hearts from harm

God hides in Nature as a thought doth hide
In humbly-sounding words ; and as the thought
Beats through the lowly word like pulse of heart
That giveth live and keepeth life alive,—
So God, thro' Nature works on ev'ry soul:
For Nature is His word so strangely writ
In Heav'n in all the letters of the stars,—
Beneath the stars in Alphabets of clouds,
And on the seas in syllables of waves,
And in the earth, on all the leaves of flowers,
And on the grasses and the stately trees,
And on the rivers and the mournful rocks
The word is clearly written,—blest are they
Who read the word aright,—and understand.

For God is everywhere—and he doth find
In every atom which His hand hath made
A shrine to hide His presence,—and reveal
His Name, Love, Power, to those who kneel
In holy faith upon this bright Below
And lift their eyes thro' all this mystery
To catch the vision of the great Beyond.

Yea! Nature is His Shadow,—and how bright
Must that face be which, such a shadow, casts?
We walk within it, for "we live and move
And have our being" in His ev'rywhere.
Why is God shy? why doth He hide Himself?
The tiniest grain of sand on ocean's shore
En-Temples Him,—the fragrance of the rose
Folds Him around as blessed incense folds
The Altars of His Christ: yet some will walk
Along the Temple's wondrous vestibule
And look, on and admire,—yet enter not

To find Within the Presence,—and the light
Which sheds its rays on all that is Without.

And Nature is His voice;—who list may hear
His Name low-murmured every—everywhere.
In song of birds,—in rustle of the flowers
In swaying of the trees,— and on the seas
The blue lips of the wavelets tell the ships
That come and go, His holy, holy name.
The winds, or still or stormy, breathe the same,
And some have ears and yet they will not hear
The soundless voice re-echoed everywhere
And some have hearts that never are enthrilled
By all the grand Hossannahs Nature sings.
List! Sanctus! Sanctus! Sanctus! without pause
Sounds sweetly out of all creation's heart
That hearts with power to love may echo back
Their Sanctus! Sanctus! Sanctus! to the **Hymn.**

PASSING AWAY,

IFE'S Vesper-bells are ringing
   In the temple of my heart,
And yon sunset, sure, is singing
   " Nunc Dimittis,"—" Now depart,"
Ah! the eve is golden-clouded
   But to-morrow's sun shall shine
On this weary body shrouded;
   But my soul doth not repine.

" Let me see the sun descending,
 I will see his light no more,
For my life, this eve, is ending
 And to-morrow on the shore
That is fair and white and golden
 I will meet my God ; and ye
Will forget not all the olden
 Happy hours ye spent with me.

" I am glad that I am going,—
 What a strange and sweet delight
Is thro' all my being flowing
 When I know that, sure, to-night
I will pass from earth and meet Him
 Whom I loved thro' all the years,
Who will crown me, when I greet Him
 And will kiss away my tears.

" My last sun ! haste ! hurry Westward !
 In the dark of this to-night
My poor soul that hastens Rest-ward
 ' With the Lamb ' will find the light ;
Death is coming—and I hear him,
 Soft and stealthy cometh he,
But I do not believe I fear him
 God is now so close to me."

  * * * * * *

Fell the daylight's fading glimmer
 On a face so wan, and white
Brighter was his soul while dimmer
 Grew the shadows of the night ;
And he died,—and God was near him
 I knelt by him to forgive ;
And I sometimes seem to hear him
 Whisper —" Live as I did live."

POETS.

POETS are strange ;—not always understood,
    By many is their gift
Which is for evil or for mighty good,—
    To lower or to lift.—

Upon their spirits there hath come a breath,—
    Who reads their verse
Will rise to higher life, or taste of death
    In blessing or in curse.

The Poet is great Nature's own High-priest,
    Ordained from very birth ;—
To keep for hearts an everlasting feast ;—
    To bless or curse the earth.

They cannot help but sing,—they know not why
    Their thoughts rush into song ;—
And float above the world beneath the sky
    For right or for the wrong.

They are like angels,—but some angels fell
    While some did keep their place ;
Their poems are the gates of Heav'n or hell—
    And God's or Satan's face

Looks thro' their ev'ry word into your face
    In blessing or in blight,
And leaves upon your soul a grace or trace
    Of sunlight or of night.—

They move along life's uttermost extremes,
    Unlike all other men,—
And in their spirits' depths sleep strangest dreams
    Like shadows in a glen.

They all are dreamers ;—in the day and night
    Ever across their souls
The wondrous mystery of the dark or bright
    In mystic rhythm rolls.

They live within themselves,—they may not tell
    What lieth deepest there ;
Within their breast, a Heaven or a hell,
    Joy or tormenting care.

They are the loneliest men that walk men's ways,
    No matter what they seem,
The stars and sunlight of their nights and days
    Move over them in dream.

They breathe it forth,—their very spirit's breath
    To bless the world, or blight,
To bring to men a higher life,—or death ;
    To give them light,—or night.

The words of some command the world's acclaim
    And never pass away,
While others' words receive no palm from fame
    And live but for a day.

But live or die,—their words leave their impress
    Fore'er or for an hour,
And mark men's souls,—some more and some the less
    With good's or evil's power.

A LEGEND.

I walked alone beside the lonely sea,
The slanting sunbeams fell upon his face,
His shadow fluttered on the pure white sands
Like the weary wing of a soundless prayer.
And he was,—oh? so beautiful and fair,—
Brown sandals on his feet,—his face downcast
As if he loved the earth more than the Heav'ns.
His face looked like his mother's,—only her's
Had not those strange serenities and stirs
That paled or flushed his olive cheeks and brow.
He wore the seamless robe his mother made;
And as he gathered it about his breast
The wavelets heard a sweet and gentle voice
Murmur "Oh! my mother;"—the white sands felt
The touch of tender tears he wept the while.
He walked beside the sea;—He took his sandals off
To bathe his weary feet in the pure cool wave,
For he had walked across the desert sands
All day long,—and as he bathed his feet
He murmured to himself,—" Three years ! three years !
And then poor feet the cruel nails will come
And make you bleed:—but ah ! that blood shall lave
All weary feet on all their thorny ways."
"Three years ! three years !" He murmured still again,
" Ah ! would it were to-morrow,—but a will,
My Father's will biddeth me bide that time."
A little fisher-boy came up the shore

And saw Him,—and, nor bold, nor shy
Approached,—but when he saw the weary face
Said mournfully to Him.—"You look a-tired."
He placed His hand upon the boy's brown brow
Caressingly and blessingly—and said
"I am so tired to wait." The boy spake not.
Sudden, a sea-bird driven by a storm
That had been sweeping on the farther shore
Came fluttering towards Him and panting fell
At His feet and died ; and then the boy said—
"Poor little bird"—in such a piteous tone,
He took the bird and laid it in His hand
And breathed on it,—when to his amaze
The little fisher-boy beheld the bird
Flutter a moment and then fly aloft—
Its little life returned,—and then he gazed
With look intensest on the wondrous face
(Ah! it was beautiful and fair)—and said
"Thou art so sweet I wish Thou wert my God."
He leaned down towards the boy and softly said
"I am thy Christ."—The day they followed Him
With cross upon His shoulders to His death,—
Within the shadow of a shelt'ring rock
That little boy knelt down,—and there adored
While others cursed the Thorn-crowned Crucified.

WHAT AILS THE WORLD?

HAT ails the world?—the Poet cried—
     " And why does Death walk everywhere?
     And why do tears fall anywhere?
     And skies have clouds, and souls have care?'
Thus the Poet sang, and sighed.

For he would fain have all things glad,
     All lives happy, all hearts bright—
     Not a day would end in night,
     Not a wrong would vex a right—
And so he sang—and he was sad.

Thro' his very grandest rhymes
     Moved a mournful monotone—
     Like a shadow Eastward thrown
     From a sunset—like a moan
Tangled in a Joy-bell's chimes.

" What ails the world?"—-he sang and asked—
     And asked and sang—but all in vain—
     No answer came to any strain,
     And no reply to his refrain—
The mystery moved 'round him masked.

" What ails the world?"—an echo came—
     ——"Ails the world?" The minstrel bands,
     With famous or forgotten hands,
     Lift up their lyres in all the lands,
And chant alike, and ask the same

From him whose soul first soared in song—
    A thousand-thousand years away,
    To him who sang but yesterday,
    In dying or in deathless lay—
"What ails the world?" comes from the throng.

    They fain would sing the world to rest—
    And so they chaunt in countless keys
    As many as the waves of seas,
    And as the breathings of the breeze,
    Yet even when they sing their best—

    When o'er the list'ning world there floats
    Such melody as 'raptures men—
    When all look up entranced—and when
    The song of fame floats forth—e'en then
A discord creepeth through the notes.

    Their sweetest harps have broken strings—
    Their grandest accords have their jars—
    Like shadows on the light of stars—
    And somehow, something ever mars
The songs the greatest minstrel sings.

    And so each song is incomplete,
    And not a rhyme can ever round
    Into the chords of perfect sound,
    The tones of thought that e'er surround
The ways walked by the Poet's feet.

"What ails the world?" he sings and sighs—
    No answer cometh to his cry—
    He asks the earth and asks the sky—
    The echoes of his song pass by
Unanswered,—and the Poet dies.

THOUGHTS.

BY sound of name, and touch of hand
    Thro' ears that hear, and eyes that see,
We know each other in this land—
    How little must that knowledge be?

Our souls are all the time alone,
    No spirit can another reach ;
They hide away in realms unknown
    Like waves that never touch a beach.

We never know each other here,
    No soul can here another see,—
To know, we need a light as clear
    As that which fills Eternity.

For here we walk by human light,
    But there the light of God is ours ;—
Each day, on earth, is but a night.
    Heaven alone hath clear-faced hours.

I call you thus,—you call me thus,—
    Our mortal is the very bar
That parts forever each of us
    As skies, on high, part star from star.

A name is nothing but a name
    For that which, else, would nameless be ;—
Until our souls, in rapture, claim
    Full knowledge in Eternity.

LINES.

HE world is sweet and fair and bright,
      And joy aboundeth everywhere,
The glorious stars crown every night
      And thro' the Dark of ev'ry care
Above us shineth Heaven's light.

If from the cradle to the grave
      We reckon all our days and hours
We, sure, will find they give and gave
      Much less of thorns and more of flowers;
And tho' some tears must ever lave

The path we tread,—upon them all
      The light of smiles forever lies
As o'er the rains, from clouds that fall
      The sun shines sweeter in the skies.
Life holdeth more of sweet than gall

For ev'ry one :—no matter who,—
      Or what their lot,—or high or low;
All hearts have clouds,—but Heaven's blue
      Wraps robes of bright around each woe ;—
And this is truest of the true,

That joy is stronger here than grief,
      Fills more of life far more of years,
And makes the reign of sorrow brief ;
      Gives more of smiles for less of tears.
Joy is life's tree,—Grief but its leaf.

THE PILGRIM.

A CHRISTMAS LEGEND FOR CHILDREN.

THE shades of night were brooding
   O'er the sea, the earth, the sky ;
The passing winds were wailing
   In a low unearthly sigh ;
The darkness gathered deeper,
   For no starry light was shed,
And silence reigned unbroken
   As the silence of the dead.

The wintry clouds were hanging
   From the starless sky so low,
While 'neath them earth lay folded
   In a winding shroud of snow.
'Twas cold—'twas dark—'twas dreary—
   And the blast that swept along
The mountains, hoarsely murmured
   A fierce, discordant song.

And mortal men were resting
   From the turmoil of the day,
And broken hearts were dreaming
   Of the friends long passed away,
And saintly men were keeping
   Their vigils through the night,
While angel spirits hovered near
   Around their lonely light.

And wicked men were sinning
    In the midnight banquet halls,
Forgetful of that sentence traced
    On proud Belshazzar's walls.
On that night so dark and dismal
    Unillumed by faintest ray,
Might be seen the lonely Pilgrim,
    Wending on his darksome way.

Slow his steps, for he was weary,
    And betimes he paused to rest ;
Then he rose, and, pressing onward,
    Murmured lowly : " I must haste."
In his hand he held a chaplet,
    And his lips were moved in prayer,
For the darkness and the silence
    Seemed to whisper, God was there.

On the lonely Pilgrim journeyed,
    Nought disturbed him on his way,
And his prayers he softly murmured,
    As the midnight stole away.
Hark ! amid the stillness rises,
    On his ears a distant strain,
Softly sounding—now it ceases—
    Sweetly now it comes again.

In his path he paused to wonder,
    While he listened to the sound :
On it came, so sweet, so pensive,
    'Mid the blast that howled around.
And the restless winds seemed soothed
    By that music, gentle, mild,
And they slept, as when a mother
    Rocks to rest her cradled child.

Strange and sweet the calm that followed
    Stealing through the midnight air ;
Strange and sweet the sounds that floated
    Like an angel breathing there.
From the sky the clouds were drifting
    Swiftly one by one away,
And the sinless stars were shedding
    Here and there a silver ray.

"Why this change?" the pilgrim whispered—
    "Whence that music? whence its power?
Earthly sounds are not so lovely !
    Angels love the midnight hour !"
Bending o'er his staff, he wondered,
    Loath to leave that sacred place :
"I must hasten," said he, sadly— •
    On he pressed with quickened pace.

Just before him rose a mountain,
    Dark its outline, steep its side—
Down its slopes that midnight music
    Seemed so soothingly to glide,
"I will find it," said the pilgrim,
    "Though this mountain I must scale,"
Scarcely said,—when on his vision
    Shone a distant light, and pale.

Glad he was ; and now he hastened—
    Brighter, brighter grew the ray—
Stronger, stronger, swelled the music,
    As he struggled on his way,
Soon he gained the mountain summit,
    Lo ! a church bursts on his view :
From the church that light was flowing,
    And that gentle music, too.

Near he came—its door stood open—
    Still he stood in awe and fear ;
" Shall I enter spot so holy ?
    Am I unforbidden here ?
I will enter—something bids me—
    Saintly men are praying here ;
Vigils sacred they are keeping,
    'Tis their matin song I hear."

Softly, noiselessly, he glided
    Through the portal—on his sight
Shone a vision, bright, strange, thrilling,
    Down he knelt—'twas Christmas night-
Down, in deepest adoration,
    Knelt the lonely Pilgrim there ;
Joy unearthly, rapture holy,
    Blended with his whispered prayer.

Wrapped his senses were in wonder,
    On his soul an awe profound,
As the vision burst upon him,
    'Mid sweet light and sweeter sound.
" Is it real ? is it earthly ?
    Is it all a fleeting dream ?
Hark ! those choral voices ringing,
    Lo ! those forms like angels seem."

On his view there rose an altar,
    Glittering 'mid a thousand beams,
Flowing from the burning tapers
    In bright, sparkling, silver streams.
From unnumbered crystal vases,
    Rose and bloomed the fairest flowers,
Shedding 'round their balmy fragrance,
    'Mid the lights in sweetest showers.

Rich and gorgeous was the altar,
  Decked it was in purest white.
Mortal hands had not arrayed it
  Thus, upon that Christmas night.
Amid its lights and lovely flowers,
  The little Tabernacle stood—
Around it all was rich and golden,
  It alone was poor and rude.

Hark ! Venite Adoremus !
  Round the golden altar sounds—
See that band of angels kneeling
  Prostrate, with their sparkling crowns !
And the Pilgrim looked and listened,
  And he saw the angels there,
And their snow-white wings were folded,
  As they bent in silent prayer.

Twelve they were—bright rays of glory
  Round their brows effulgent shone ;
But a wreath of nobler beauty
  Seemed to grace and circle one ;
And he, beauteous, rose and opened
  Wide the Tabernacle door :
Hark ! " Venite Adoremus "
  Rises—bending, they adore.

Lo ! a sound of censers swinging !
  Clouds of incense weave around
The altar rich a silver mantle,
  As the angels' hymns resound.
List ! Venite Adoremus
  Swells aloud in stronger strains,
And the angels swing the censers,
  And they prostrate bend again.

Rising now, with voice of rapture,
　　Bursts aloud, in thrilling tone,
" Gloria in Excelsis Deo "
　　Round the sacramental throne.
Oh ! 'twas sweet, 'twas sweet and charming
　　As the notes triumphant flowed !
Oh ! 'twas sweet, while wreaths of incense
　　Curled, and countless tapers glowed.

Oh ! 'twas grand ! that hymn of glory
　　Earthly sounds cannot compare ;
Oh ! 'twas grand ! it breath'd of Heaven,
　　As the angels sung it there.
Ravished by the strains ecstatic,
　　Raptured by the vision grand,
Gazed the Pilgrim on the altar,
　　Gazed upon the angel band.

All was hushed ! the floating echoes
　　Of the hymn had died away ;
Vanished were the clouds of incense,
　　And the censers ceased to sway.
Lo ! their wings are gently waving,
　　And the angels softly rise,
Bending towards the Tabernacle,
　　Worship beaming from their eyes.

One last, lowly genuflection !
　　From their brows love burning shone—
Ah, they're going, they've departed,
　　All but one, the brightest one.
" Why remains he ? " thought the Pilgrim,
　　Ah ! he rises beauteously—
" Listen ! " and the angel murmured
　　Sweetly : " Pilgrim, hail to thee ! "

" Come unto the golden altar,
  I'm an angel—banish fear—
Come, unite in adoration
  With me, for our God is here.
Come ! thy Jesus here reposes,
  Come ! He'll bless thy mortal sight—
Come ! adore the Infant Saviour
  With me—for 'tis Christmas night."

Now approached the Pilgrim, trembling,
  Now beside the angel bent,
And the deepest, blissful gladness,
  With his fervent worship blent.
" Pilgrim," said the spirit, softly,
  " 'Thou hast seen bright angels here,
And hast heard our sacred anthems,
  Filled with rapture, filled with fear.

" We are twelve—'twas we who chanted
  First the Saviour's lowly birth,
We who brought the joyful tidings
  Of His coming, to the earth ;
We who sung unto the Shepherds,
  Watching on the mountain hight,
That the Word was made Incarnate,
  For them on that blessed night.

" And since then we love to linger,
  On that festal night on earth,
And we leave our thrones of glory
  Here to keep the Saviour's birth.
Happy mortals ! happy mortals !
  To-night the angels would be men ;
And they leave their thrones in Heaven
  For the Crib of Bethlehem."

And the angel led the Pilgrim
 To the Tabernacle door;
Lo! an infant there was sleeping,
 And the angel said, "Adore!
He is sleeping yet He watches,
 See that beam of love divine,
Pilgrim! pay your worship holy
 To your infant God and mine."

And the spirit slowly, slowly,
 Closed the Tabernacle door,
While the Pilgrim lowly, lowly,
 Bent in rapture to adore.
"Pilgrim," spoke the angel sweetly,
 "I must bid thee my adieu;
Love! oh, love the Infant Jesus!"--
 And he vanished from his view.

* * * * * * *

All was silent,—silent—silent —
 Faded was the vision bright—
But the Pilgrim long remembered,
 In his heart, that Christmas night.

WO little children played among the flowers,
Their mothers were of kin, tho' far apart ;
The children's ages were the very same
E'en to an hour ;—and Ethel was her name,—
A fair, sweet girl, with great, brown, wond'ring eyes
That seemed to listen just as if they held
The gift of hearing with the power of sight.
Six summers slept upon her low white brow
And dreamed amid the roses of her cheeks.
Her voice was sweetly low ;—and when she spoke
Her words were music ; and her laughter rang
So like an Altar-bell that, had you heard
Its silvery sound a-ringing,—you would think
Of kneeling down and worshiping the Pure.

They played among the roses,—it was May,—
And "hide and seek," and "seek and hide," all eve
They played together till the sun went down.
Earth held no happier hearts than theirs that day :
And tired at last she plucked a crimson rose
And gave to him, her playmate, cousin-kin ;—
And he went thro' the garden till he found
The whitest rose of all the roses there,
And placed it in her long, brown, waving hair.
" I give you red,—and you,—you give me white :
What is the meaning ?"—said she,—while a smile
As radiant as the light of angel's wings,
Swept bright across her face ;—the while her eyes

Seemed infinite purities half asleep
In sweetest pearls :—and he did make reply
" Sweet Ethel ! White dies first,—you know, the snow,
(And it is not as white as thy pure face)
Melts soon away,—but roses red as mine
Will bloom when all the snow hath passed away."

She sighed a little sigh,—then laughed again,—
And hand in hand they walked the winding ways
Of that fair garden till they reached her home.
A good-bye and a kiss,—and he was gone.

She leaned her head upon her mother's breast,
And ere she fell asleep she, sighing, called,
" Does White die first ? my mother ! and does Red
Live longer ? "—and her mother wondered much
At such strange speech.   She fell asleep
With murmurs on her lips of Red and White.
Those children loved as only children can,
With nothing in their love save their whole selves,
When in their cradles they had been betroth'd.
They knew it in a manner vague and dim,—
Unconscious yet of what betrothal meant.

The boy—she called him Merlin—a love-name,—
(And he—he called her always Ullainee,
No matter why ;)—the boy was full of moods.
Upon his soul and face the Dark and Bright
Were strangely intermingled.   Hours would pass
Rippling with his bright prattle,—and then, hours
Would come and go ; and never hear a word
Fall from his lips,—and never see a smile
Upon his face.   He was so like a cloud
With ever-changeful hues, as she was like
A golden sunbeam shining on its face.

*   *   *   *   *   *   *   *

Ten years passed on.   They parted and they met
Not often in each year,—yet as they grew
In years, a consciousness unto them came
Of human love.
    But it was sweet and pure.
There was no passion in it.   Reverence
Like Guardian-Angel watched o'er Innocence.
One night in mid of May their faces met
As pure as all the stars that gazed on them.
They met to part from themselves and the world.
Their hearts just touched to separate and bleed,
Their eyes were linked in look, while saddest tears
Fell down like rain upon the cheeks of each :
They were to meet no more.
    Their hands were clasped.
To tear the clasp in twain ; and all the stars
Looked proudly down on them, while shadows knelt
Or seemed to kneel around them with the awe
Evoked from any heart by sacrifice.
And in the heart of that last, parting hour
Eternity was beating.   And he said,
" We part to go to Calvary and to God,—
This is our Garden of Gethsemane;
And here we bow our heads and breathe His prayer
Whose heart was bleeding, while the angels heard :
Not My will, Father! but Thine Own be done."

Raptures meet agonies in such Heart-hours ;
Gladness doth often fling her bright, warm arms
Around the cold, white neck of grief ;—and thus
The while they parted—sorrow swept their hearts
Like a great, dark stormy sea,—but sudden
A joy, like sunshine,—did it come from God?

Flung over every wave that swept o'er them
A more than golden glory.

          Merlin said:

" Our loves must soar aloft to spheres Divine,
The Human satisfies nor you nor me,
(No human love shall ever satisfy,—
Or ever did,—the hearts that lean on it ;)
You sigh for something higher as do I,
So let our spirits be espoused in God,
And let our wedlock be as soul to soul ;
And Prayer shall be the golden Marriage-ring
And God will bless us both."

          She sweetly said :

" Your words are echoes of my own soul's thoughts;
Let God's own heart be our own holy home,
And let us live as only angels live ;
And let us love as our own angels love.
'Tis hard to part,—but it is better so,
God's will is ours, and,—Merlin ! let us go."

And then she sobbed as if her heart would break,—
Perhaps it did ;—an awful minute passed,
Long as an age and briefer than a flash
Of lightning in the skies.   No word was said ;
Only a look which never was forgot.
Between them fell the shadows of the night.

Their faces went away into the dark,
And never met again ; and yet their souls
Were twined together in the heart of Christ.

And Ethel went from earthland long ago,
But Merlin stays still hanging on his cross.
He would not move a nail that nails him there,
He would not pluck a thorn that crowns him there.

He hung himself upon the blessed cross
With Ethel ;—she has gone to wear the crown
That wreathes the brows of virgins who have kept
Their bodies with their souls from earthly taint.

And years and years, and weary years passed on
Into the Past ;—one Autumn afternoon,
When flowers were in their agony of death,
And winds sang " De Profundis " over them,
And skies were sad with shadows,—he did walk
Where, in a resting-place as calm as sweet,—
The dead were lying down ;—the Autumn sun
Was half way down the West,—the hour was three,
The holiest hour of all the Twenty-four,—
For Jesus leaned His head on it—and died.
He walked alone amid the virgins' graves,
Where virgins slept,—a convent stood near by,
And from the solitary cells of nuns
Unto the cells of death the way was short.

Low, simple stones and white watched o'er each grave,
While in the hollows 'tween them sweet flowers grew
Entwining grave with grave.   He read the names
Engraven on the stones,—and " Rest in Peace."
Was written 'neath them all—and o'er each name
A Cross was graven on the lowly stone.
He passed each grave with reverential awe,
As if he passed an Altar, where the Host
Had left a memory of its sacrifice.
And o'er the buried virgins' virgin dust
He walked as prayerfully as tho' he trod
The holy floor of fair Loretto's shrine.
He passed from grave to grave,—and read the names
Of those whose own pure lips had changed the names

By which this world had known them, into names
Of sacrifice known only to their God :
Veiling their faces they had veiled their names.
The very ones who played with them as girls,
Had they passed there would know no more than he,
Or any stranger, where their playmates slept.
And then he wondered all about their lives, their hearts,
Their thoughts, their feelings, and their dreams,
Their joys and sorrows, and their smiles and tears.
He wondered at the stories that were hid
Forever down within those simple graves.

In a lone corner of that resting-place
Uprose a low, white slab that marked a grave—
Apart from all the others :—long, sad grass
Drooped o'er the little mound, and mantled it
With veil of purest green,—around the slab
The whitest of white roses 'twined their arms,
Roses cold as the snows and pure as songs
Of angels,—and the pale leaflets and thorns
Hid e'en the very name of her who slept
Beneath.   He walked on to the grave, but when
He reached its side, a spell fell on his heart,
So suddenly,—he knew not why,—and tears
Went up into his eyes and trickled down
Upon the grass ;—he was as strangely moved
As if he met a long-gone face he loved.
I believe he prayed.   He lifted then the leaves
That hid the name ;—but as he did, the thorns
Did pierce his hand ;—and lo ! amazed he read
The very word,—the very, very name
He gave the girl in golden days before,—
                "Ullainee."
He sat beside that lonely grave, for long,

He took its grasses in his trembling hand,—
He toyed with them, and wet them with his tears,—
He read the name again and still again,
He thought a thousand thoughts. — and then he thought
It all might be a dream,—then rubbed his eyes
And read the name again to be more sure,
Then wondered and then wept,—then asked himself :
" What means it all ?   Can this be Ethel's grave ?
I dreamed her soul had fled.
Was she the white dove that I saw in dream
Fly o'er the sleeping sea so long ago ? "
                    The convent-bell
Rang sweet upon the breeze, and answered him
His question.   And he rose and went his way
Unto the convent gate ; long shadows marked
One hour before the sunset ; and the birds
Were singing Vespers in the convent trees.
As silent as a star-gleam came a nun
In answer to his summons at the gate ;
Her face was like the picture of a saint,
Or like an angel's smile ;—her downcast eyes
Were like a half-closed Tabernacle, where
God's presence glowed,—her lips were pale and worn
By ceaseless prayer,—and when she sweetly spoke
And bade him enter,—'twas in such a tone
As only voices own which day and night
Sing hymns to God.
                    She locked the massive gate.
He followed her along a flower-fringed walk
That, gently rising, led up to the Home
Of Virgin-Hearts.   The very flowers that bloomed
Within the place, in beds of sacred shapes,—
(For they had fashioned them with holy care,

Into all holy forms,—a Chalice, a Cross,
And Sacred Hearts,—and many saintly names,
That when their eyes would fall upon the flowers
Their souls might feast upon some mystic sign),—
Were fairer far within the convent walls,
And purer in their fragrance and their bloom
Than all their sisters in the outer world.

He went into a wide and humble room,
The floor was painted ;—and upon the walls
In humble frames most holy paintings hung.
Jesus and Mary and many an olden Saint
Were there.   And she, the veil-clad sister, spoke :
" I'll call the Mother,"—and she bowed and went.

He waited in the wide and humble room,—
The only room in that unworldly place
This world could enter,—and the pictures looked
Upon his face and down into his soul
And strangely stirred him.   On the mantel stood
A crucifix, the figured Christ of which
Did seem to suffer ; and he rose to look
More nearly on it ; but he shrank in awe
When he beheld a something in its face
Like his own face.——
But more amazed he grew, when, at the foot
Of that strange crucifix he read the name,—

"ULLAINEE."

A whirl of thought swept o'er his startled soul,—
When to the door he heard a footstep come,
And then a voice ;—the Mother of the nuns
Had entered,—and in calmest tone began :
" Forgive, kind sir, my stay ;—our Matin-song
Had not yet ended when you came ;—our rule

Forbids our leaving choir ;—this, my excuse."
She bent her head,—the rustle of her veil
Was like the trembling of an angel's wing,
Her voice's tone as sweet.   She turned to him
And seemed to ask him with her still, calm look
What brought him there,—and waited his reply.
" I am a stranger, Sister, hither come,"
He said, "upon an errand still more strange.
But thou wilt pardon me and bid me go,
If what I crave, you cannot rightly grant,—
I would not dare intrude, nor claim your time
Save that a friendship, deep as death, and strong
As life, has brought me to this holy place."

He paused.   She looked at him an instant,—bent
Her lustrous eyes upon the floor,—but gave
Him no reply,—save that her very look
Encouraged him to speak,—and he went on :
He told her Ethel's story from the first,
He told her of the day amid the flowers,
When they were only six sweet summers old ;
He told her of the night when all the flowers,
A -listning, heard the words of sacrifice,
He told her all ;—then said : "I saw a stone
In yonder graveyard where your sisters sleep,
And writ on it, all hid by roses white,
I saw a name I never ought forget."

She wore a startled look,—but soon repressed
The wonder that had come into her face.
" Whose name ?" she calmly spoke.   But when he said :

" ULLAINEE,"

She forward bent her face and pierced his own

With look intensest ;—and he thought he heard
The trembling of her veil,—as if the brow
It mantled, throbbed with many thrilling thoughts.
But quickly rose she, and in hurried tone
Spoke thus : " 'Tis hour of sunset,—'tis our rule
To close the gates to all till morrow's morn.
Return to-morrow,—then, if so God wills,
I'll see you."

　　　　　　　He gave many thanks, passed out
From that unworldly place into the world.
Straight to the lonely graveyard went his steps,
Swift to the " White-Rose-Grave," his heart : he knelt
Upon its grass and prayed that God might will
The mystery's solution ;—then he took,—
Where it was drooping on the slab, a rose,—
The whiteness of whose leaves was like the foam
Of summer waves upon a summer sea.

　　　　　　　Then thro' the night he went
And reached his room where, weary of his thoughts,
Sleep came, and coming found the dew of tears
Undried within his eyes,—and flung her veil
Around him.　Then he dreamt a strange, weird dream.
A rock, dark waves, white roses and a grave,
And cloistered flowers, and cloistered nuns,—and tears
That shone like jewels on a diadem,—
And two great angels with such shining wings ;
All these and more were, in most curious way,
Blended in one dream or many dreams.　Then
He woke wearier in his mind.　Then slept
Again and had another dream.
His dream ran thus,—
(He told me all of it many years ago,

But I forgot the most.   I remember this} :
A dove whiter than whitness' very self
Fluttered thro' his sleep in vision or dream,
Bearing in its flight a spotless rose.   It
Flew away across great, long distances,
Thro' forests where the trees were all in-dream,
And over wastes where silences held reign,
And down pure valleys, till it reached a shore,
By which blushed a sea in the ev'ning sun ;
The dove rested there awhile ;—rose again
And flew across the sea into the sun.
And then from near or far (he could not say)
Came sound as faint as echo's own echo,—
A low sweet hymn it seemed,—and now
And then he heard, or else he thought he heard,
As if it were the hymn's refrain,—the words,
" White dies first ! " " White dies first."—

The sun had passed his noon and Westward sloped ;—
He hurried to the cloister and was told
The mother waited him.   He entered in
Into the wide and pictured room,—and there
The Mother sat,—and gave him welcome twice.
" I prayed, last night," she spoke, "to know God's will,
I prayed to Holy Mary and the Saints
That they might pray for me,—and I might know
My conduct in the matter ;—now, kind sir,
What would'st thou ?   Tell thy errand."   He replied :
" It was not idle curiosity
That brought me hither or that prompts my lips
To ask the story of the White-Rose-Grave,—
To seek the story of the sleeper there,
Whose name I knew so long and far away.
Who was she pray ?   Dost deem it right to tell ? "

There was a pause before the answer came,—
As if there was a comfort in her heart.
There was a tremor in her voice when she
Unclosed two palest lips,—and spoke in tone
Of whisper more than word.
                    " She was a child
Of lofty gift and grace, who fills that grave,
And who has filled it long,—and yet it seems
To me but one short hour ago, we laid
Her body there.   Her mem'ry clings around
Our hearts, our cloister,—fresh and fair and sweet.
We often look for her in places where
Her face was wont to be ;—among the flow'rs,
In chapel,—underneath those trees.   Long years
Have passed and mouldered her pure face : and yet
It seems to hover here and haunt us all.
I can not tell you all.   It is enough
To see one ray of light—for us to judge
The glory of the sun ;—it is enough
To catch one glimpse of heaven's blue,
For us to know the beauty of the sky.
It is enough to tell a little part
Of her most holy life that you may know
The hidden grace and splendor of the whole.
" Nay,—nay."   He interrupted her—"all ! all !
Thou'lt tell me all, kind mother."

              •   She went on,
Unheeding his abruptness.
                    "One sweet day,—
A feast of Holy Virgin,—in the month
Of May—at early morn, e're yet the dew
Had passed from off the flowers and grass,—e're yet
Our nuns had come from holy Mass,—there came

With summons quick unto our Convent gate
A fair young girl.   Her feet were wet with dew,—
Another dew was moist within her eyes,—
Her large, brown, wond'ring eyes.   She asked for me,
And as I went she rushed into my arms
Like weary bird into the leaf-roofed branch
That sheltered it from storm.   She sobbed and sobbed,
Until I thought her very soul would rush
From her frail body, in a sob, to God
I let her sob her sorrow all away.
My words were waiting for a calm.   Her sobs
Sank into sighs,—and they too sank and died
In faintest breath.   I bore her to a seat
In this same room,—and gently spoke to her.
And held her hand in mine,—and soothed her
With words of sympathy, until she seemed
As tranquil as myself.

            And then I asked ;
What brought thee hither, child, and what wilt thou ?
' Mother !' she said ;—' Wilt let me wear the veil?
Wilt let me serve my God as e'en you serve
Him in this cloistered place ?   I pray to be,—
Unworthy tho' I be,—to be his spouse.
Nay, Mother—say not nay—'twill break a heart
Already broken ; "—and she looked on me
With those brown, wond'ring eyes which pleaded more,
More strongly and more sadly than her lips
That I might grant her sudden, strange request.
' Hast thou a mother ?' questioned I.   ' I had,'
She said—' but heaven has her now ;—and thou
Wilt be my mother,—and the orphan girl
Will make her life her thanks.'

'Thy father, child?'
'Ere I was cradled he was in his grave.'
'And hast nor sister nor brother?' 'No,'—she said,
'God gave my mother only me ;—one year
   This very day he parted us.' 'Poor child'—
I murmured,—'Nay—kind sister'—she replied :
'I have much wealth,—they left me ample means,—
I have true friends who love me and protect.
I was a minor until yesterday ;
But yesterday all guardianship did cease,
And I am mistress of myself and all
My worldly means,—and Sister, they are thine
If thou but take myself,—nay—don't refuse.'
'Nay—nay—my child?' I said,—'The only wealth
   We wish for is the wealth of soul—of grace.
Not all your gold could unlock yonder gate,
Or buy a single thread of virgin's veil.
Not all the coins in coffers of a king
Could bribe an entrance here for any one.
God's voice alone can claim a cell,—a veil,
   For any one he sends.
                        Who sent you here,
My child? Thyself? Or did some holy one
Direct thy steps? Or else some sudden grief?
Or mayhap, disappointment? Or perhaps,
A sickly weariness of that bright world
   Hath cloyed thy spirit? Tell me, which it is.'
'Neither'—she quickly, almost proudly spoke.
'Who sent you then?'
                        'A youthful Christ'—she said·
'Who, had he lived in those far days of Christ
   Would have been His belov'd Disciple, sure,
   Would have been His own gentle John ; and would

Have leaned, on Thursday night, upon his breast
And stood, on Friday eve, beneath His cross
To take His Mother from Him when He died.
He sent me here,—he said the word last night
In my own garden,—this the word he said :
Oh ! had you heard him whisper : 'Ethel dear !
Your heart was born with veil of virgin on,—
I hear it rustle every time we meet,
In all your words and smiles ;—and when you weep
I hear it rustle more. Go—wear your veil,—
And outward be what inwardly thou art,
And hast been from the first. And, Ethel, list !
My heart was born with priestly vestments on,
And at Dream-Altars I have ofttimes stood,
And said such sweet Dream-Masses in my sleep,—
And when I lifted up a white Dream-Host,
A silver Dream-Bell rang,—and angels knelt,
Or seemed to kneel in worship. Ethel, say—
Thou would'st not take the vestments from my heart
No more than I would tear the veil from thine.
My vested and thy veiled heart part to-night
To climb our Calvary and to meet in God,—
And this,—fair Ethel ! is Gethsemane,—
And He is here, Who, in that other, bled,—
And they are here who came to comfort Him,—
His angels and our own ;—and His great prayer,
Ethel, is ours to-night ;—let's say it then :
Father ! thy will be done ! Go find your veil
And I my vestments,'—He did send me here.' "

" She paused,—a few stray tears had dropped upon
Her closing words and softened them to sighs.
I listened, inward moved,—but outward, calm and cold,
To the girl's strange story. Then smiling said :

'I see it is a love-tale after all,
With much of folly and some of fact in it,—
It is a heart-affair, and in such things
There's little logic, and there's less of sense.
You brought your heart, dear child, but left your head
Outside the gates,—nay! go, and find the head
You lost last night,—and then, I am quite sure,
You'll not be anxious to confine your heart
Within this cloistered place.'
                            She seemed to wince
Beneath my words, one moment ;—then replied :
' If e'en a wounded heart did bring me here,
Dost thou do, Sister, well, to wound it more ?
If merely warmth of feelings urged me here
Dost thou do well to chill them into ice ?
And were I disappointed in yon world
Should that debar me from a purer place?
You say it is a love tale—so it is ;—
The vase was human—but the flower divine,
And if I break the vase with my own hands
Will you forbid that I should humbly ask
The heart of God to be my lily's vase ?
I'd trust my lily to no heart on earth
Save his, who yester-night, did send me here
To dip it in the very blood of Christ,
And plant it here.'
                    "And then she sobbed outright
A long, deep sob.
                    I gently said to her:
' Nay—child—I spoke to test thee,—do not weep.
If thou art called of God, thou yet shalt come
And find e'en here a home.   But God is slow
In all His works and ways, and slower still

When He would deck a bride to grace His Court.
Go, now, and in one year;—if thou dost come
Thy veil and cell shall be prepared for thee—
'Nay—urge me not—it is our holy rule,—
A year of trial! I must to choir, and thou
Into the world to watch and wait and pray
Until the Bridegroom comes.'
             She rose and went
Without a word.

             And twelvemonth after came,
True to the very day and hour ;—and said :
' Wilt keep thy promise made one year ago ?
Where is my cell—and where my virgin's veil ?'
Wilt try me more ? Wilt send me back again?
I came once with my wealth and was refused,
And now I come as poor as Holy Christ
Who had no place to rest his weary head,—
My wealth is gone ; I offered it to him
Who sent me here ;—he sent me speedy word ;—
' Give all unto the poor in quiet way
And hide the giving—ere you give yourself
To God !' Wilt take me now for my own sake?
I bring my soul,—'tis little worth I ween,—
And yet it cost sweet Christ a priceless price.'

' My child,' I said, ' thrice welcome ;—enter here ;
A few short days of silence and of prayer
And thou shalt be the Holy Bridegroom's Bride.'

Her novice days went on ; much sickness fell
Upon her. Oft she lay for weary weeks
In awful agonies,—and no one heard
A murmur from her lips. She oft would smile

A sunny, playful smile that she might hide
Her sufferings from us all.   When she was well,
She was the first to meet the hour of prayer,—
The last to leave it,—and they named her well,
The Angel of the Cloister.   Once I heard
The Father of our souls say, when she passed,—
' Beneath that veil of sacrificial black
She wears the white robe of her innocence.'
And we,—we believed it.   There are Sisters here
Of three score years of service, who would say :
' Within our mem'ry never moved a veil
That hid so saintly and so pure a heart.'
And we, we felt it,—and we loved her so,
We treated her as angel and as child.
I never heard her speak about the past,
I never heard her mention e'en a name
Of any in the world.   She little spake.
She seemed to have rapt moments—then she grew
Absent-minded,—and would come and ask me
To walk alone and say her Rosary
Beneath the trees.   She had a voice divine,
And when she sang for us, in truth it seemed
The very heart of song was breaking on her lips.
The dower of her mind, as of her heart,
Was of the richest, and she mastered art
By instinct more than study.   Her weak hands
Moved ceaselessly amid the beautiful.
There is a picture hanging in our choir
She painted.   I remember well the morn
She came to me and told me she had dreampt
A dream ; then asked me would I let her paint
Her dream.   I gave permission.   Weeks and weeks
Went by,—and ev'ry spare hour of the day

She kept her cell all busy with her work.
At last 'twas finished and she brought it forth.
A picture my poor words may not portray,
But you must gaze on it with your own eyes
And drink its magic and its meanings in ;
I'll show it thee, kind sir, before you go.

In every May for two whole days she kept
Her cell. We humored her in that, but when
The days had passed,—and she came forth again,
Her face was tender as a lily's leaf
With God's smile on it,—and for days and days
Thereafter,—she would scarcely ope her lips
Save when in prayer,—and then her every look
Was rapt as if her soul did hold with God
Strange converse. And who knows ? mayhap she did.

I half forgot.—On yonder mantelpiece
You see that wondrous crucifix,—one year
She spent on it, and begged to put beneath
That most mysterious word : ' Ullainee."—

At last the Cloister's Angel disappeared,
Her face was missed at choir,—her voice was missed,
Her words were missed where every day we met
In recreation's hour.   And those who passed
The Angel's cell would lightly tread—and breathe
A prayer that Death might pass the Angel by
And let her longer stay, for she lay ill,
Her frail, pure life was ebbing fast away.

Ah ! many were the orisons that rose
From all our hearts that God might spare her still.
At Benediction and at holy Mass
Our hands were lifted, and strong pleadings went

To Heaven for her ; we did love her so,
Perhaps too much we loved her ; and perhaps
Our love was far too human.   Slow and slow
She faded like a flower.   And slow and slow
Her pale cheeks whitened more.   And slow and slow
Her large, brown wondering eyes sank deep and dim.
Hope died in all our faces—but on her's
Another and a different Hope did shine,
And from her wasted lips sweet prayers arose
That made her watchers weep.   Fast came the end.
Never such silence o'er the Cloister hung :
We walked more softly, and whene'er we spoke
Our voices fell to whispers—lest a sound
Might jar upon her ear.   The Sisters watched
In turns beside her couch.   To each she gave
A gentle word,—a smile,—a thankful look.
At times her mind did wander ; no wild words
Escaped her lips ; she seemed to float away
To far-gone days and live again in scenes
Whose hours were bright and happy.   In her sleep
She ofttimes spoke low, gentle, holy words
About her mother.   And sometimes she sang
The fragments of sweet, olden songs,—and when
She woke again, she timidly would ask
If she had spoken in her sleep—and what
She said,—as if, indeed, her heart did fear
That sleep might open there some long-closed gate
She would keep locked.   And softly as a cloud,
A golden cloud upon a summer's day,
Floats from the heart of land out o'er the sea—
So her sweet life was passing.   One bright eve,
The fourteenth day of August, when the sun
Was wrapping, like a king, a purple cloud

Around him,—on descending day's bright throne,
She sent for me and bade me come in haste.
I went into her cell.   There was a light
Upon her face, unearthly ; and it shone
Like gleam of star upon a dying rose.
I sat beside her couch,—and took her hand
In mine,—a fair, frail hand that scarcely seem'd
Of flesh,—so wasted, white and wan it was.
Her great, brown, wond'ring eyes had sunk away
Deep in their sockets,—and their light shone dim
As tapers dying on an Altar.   Soft
As a dream of beauty on me fell, low,
Last words.

     'Mother ! the tide is ebbing **fast** ;
But e're it leaves this shore to cross the deep
And seek another, calmer—I would say
A few last words,—and, mother, I would ask
One favor more, which thou wilt not refuse.
Thou wert a mother to the orphan-girl,
Thou gav'st her heart a home,—her love, a vase,—
Her weariness, a rest,—her sacrifice, a shrine,—
And thou did'st love me, Mother, as she loved
Whom I shall meet to-morrow. far away,—
But no,—it is not far,—that other Heav'n
Touches this,—Mother ! I have felt its touch,
And now I feel its clasp upon my soul.
I'm going from this heaven into that,
To-morrow, Mother.   Yes—I dreamt it all.
It was the sunset of Our Lady's feast.
My soul passed upwards thro' the golden clouds
To sing the second Vespers of the day
With all the Angels.   Mother—'ere I go—
Thou'lt listen. Mother sweet, to my last words.

Which, like all last words, tell what e'er was first
In life or tenderest in heart. I came
Unto my convent cell and virgin veil,
Sent by a spirit that had touched mine own
As wings of angels touch,—to fly apart
Upon their missions—till they meet again
In Heaven, heart to heart, wing to wing.
The 'Angel of the Cloister,' you called me,
Unworthy sure of such a beauteous name,—
My mission's over—and your Angel goes
To-morrow home. This earthly part which stays
You'll lay away within a simple grave,—
But Mother, on its slab thou'lt grave this name,
Ullainee;' (She spelt the letters out).
Nor ask me why,—tho' if thou wilt, I'll tell;
It is my soul-name, given long ago
By one who found it in some Eastern book
Or dreamt it in a dream and gave it me,
Nor ever told the meaning of the name;—
And, Mother, should he ever come and read
That name upon my grave, and come to thee
And ask thee tidings of Ullainee,
Thou'lt tell him all,—and watch him if he weeps,—
Show him the crucifix my poor hands carved,—
Show him the picture in the chapel choir,—
And watch him if he weeps,—and then
There are three humble scrolls in yonder drawer,'—
(She pointed to the table in her room)
'Some words of mine and words of his are there.
And keep these simple scrolls until he comes,
And put them in his hands;—and, Mother, watch,
Watch him if he weeps;—and tell him this,—
I tasted all the sweets of sacrifice,

I kissed my cross a thousand times a day,
I hung and bled upon it in my dreams,
I lived on it—I loved it to the last.'   And then
A low, soft sigh crept thro' the Virgin's cell,—
I looked upon her face,—and death was there."
There was a pause,—and in the pause one wave
Of shining tears swept thro' the Mother's eyes.
And thus," she said, "our Angel passed away.
We buried her,—and at her last request
We wrote upon the slab, ' Ullainee.'
And I,—(for she had asked me one day thus,
The day she hung her picture in the choir)
I planted o'er her grave a white rose tree.
The roses crept around the slab and hid
The graven name,—and still, we sometimes cull
Her sweet, white roses, and we place them on
Our Chapel-Altar."
                    Then the Mother rose,
Without another word, and led him thro'
A long, vast hall,—then up a flight of stairs
Unto an oaken door, which turned upon its hinge
Noiselessly,—then into a Chapel dim,—
On Gospel-side of which there was a gate
From ceiling down to floor,—and back of that
A long and narrow choir, with many stalls,
Brown-oaken ; all along the walls were hung
Saint-pictures, whose sweet faces looked upon
The faces of the Sisters in their prayers.
Beside a "Mater Dolorosa" hung
The picture of the "Angel of the choir."
He sees it now thro' vista of the years,
Which stretch between him and that long-gone day,
It hangs within his memory as fresh

In tint and touch and look as long ago.
There was a power in it, as if the soul
Of her who painted it had shrined in it
Its very self ; there was a spell in it
That fell upon his spirit thro' his eyes,
And made him dream of God's own holy heart.
The shadow of the picture, in weak words,
Was this,—or something very like to this :
———— A wild, wierd wold,
Just like the desolation of a heart,—
Stretched far away into infinity ;
Above it low, gray skies drooped sadly down
As if they fain would weep,—and all was bare
As bleakness' own bleak self ;—a mountain stood
All mantled with the glory of a light
That flashed from out the heavens,—and a Cross
With such a pale Christ hanging in its arms
Did crown the mount ;—and either side the Cross
There were two crosses lying on the rocks,—
One of whitest roses;—ULLAINEE   ·
Was woven into it with buds of red ;—
And one of reddest roses;—Merlin's name
Was woven into it with buds of white.
Below the Cross and Crosses and the mount
The earth-place lay so dark and bleak and drear,
Above,—a golden glory seemed to hang
Like God's own benediction o'er the names.

I saw the picture once ;—it moved me so
I nee'r forgot its beauty or its truth;
But words as weak as mine can never paint
That Crucifixion's picture.

Merlin said to me,
'Some day—some far off day when I am dead,
You have the simple rhymings of two hearts,
And if you think it best,—the world may know
A love-tale crowned by purest SACRIFICE."

LINES.

HE death of men is not the death
Of Rights that urged them to the fray;
  For men may yield
  On battle field
A noble life with stainless shield,
  And swords may rust
  Above their dust,—
  But still,—and still
  The touch and thrill
Of Freedom's vivifying breath
Will nerve a heart and rouse a will
In some hour in the days to be,
To win back triumphs from defeat,
And those who blame us,—then will greet
Right's glorious eternity.

For Right lives in a thousand things;
  Its cradle is its martyr's grave,
Wherein it rests awhile until,
  The life that heroisms gave

Will rise again, at God's own will,
    And right the wrong
    Which long and long,
Did reign above the true and just ;—
And thro' the songs the poet sings.
Right's vivifying spirit rings ;
    Each simple rhyme
    Keeps step and time
With those who marched away and fell,
    And all his lines,
    Are humble shrines,
Where love of Right will love to dwell.

———

DEATH OF THE PRINCE IMPERIAL.

WAILETH a woman "Oh! my God!"
A breaking heart in a broken breath.—
A hopeless cry o'er her heart-hope's death !
Can words catch the chords of the winds that wail,
When love's last lily lies dead in the vale ?
    Let her alone,
    Under the rod
    With the infinite moan
    Of her soul for God.
Ah ! song ! you may echo the sound of pain,
    But you never may shrine,
    In verse or line,
The pang of the heart that breaks in twain.

Waileth a woman,—Oh ! my God !
Wind-driven waves with no hearts that ache,
Why do your passionate pulses throb?
No lips that speak,—have ye souls that sob?
We carry the cross,—ye wear the crest,
We have our God, — and ye, your shore,
Whither ye rush in the storm to rest ;
We have the havens of holy prayer,—
And we have a Hope,—have ye despair?
For storm-rocked waves ye break evermore,
Adown the shores and along the years,
In the whitest foam of the saddest tears,
And we, as ye, oh? waves, gray waves!
Drift over a sea more deep and wide,
For we have sorrow and we have death,
And ye have only the tempest's breath;
But we have God when heart-oppressed,
As a calm and beautiful shore of rest.

Oh waves ! sad waves ! how you flowed between
The crownless Prince and the exiled Queen !

Waileth a woman ! oh ! my God !
Her hopes are withered—her heart is crushed,
For the Love of her love is cold and dead, .
The Joy of her joy hath forever fled ;
A starless and pitiless night hath rushed
On the Light of her life,— and far away
In an Afric wild lies her poor dead child,
Lies the Heart of her heart,—let her alone
        Under the rod
           With her infinite moan,
       Oh ! my God !

He was beautiful, pure and brave,
        The brightest grace
        Of a royal race ;—
Only his throne is but a grave ;
        Is there fate in fames?
        Is there doom in names?
Ah! what did the cruel Zulu-spears
Care for the Prince or his mother's tears?
What did the Zulu's ruthless lance
Care for the Hope of the future France?

Crieth the Empress—"Oh! my son!"
He was her own and her only one,
She had nothing to give him but her love,
'Twas kingdom enough on earth,—Above
She gave him an infinite faith in God ;—
    Let her cry her cry
Over her own and only one,
All the glory is gone—is gone,
    Into her broken-hearted sigh.

Moaneth a mother,—"Oh! my child!"
And who can sound that depth of woe?
Homeless,—throneless, crownless, now
She bows her sorrow-wreathed brow,—
(So Fame and all its grandeurs go)
        Let her alone
        Beneath the rod
        With her infinite moan,
        Oh! my God.

O words of mine ! and if you live
    Only for one brief, little day;
If peace, or joy, or calm you give
    To any soul ;—or if you bring
A something higher to some heart,
    I may come back again and sing
Songs free from all the arts of Art.

RETURN
TO ➡

CIRCULATION DEPARTMENT
202 Main Library

LOAN PERIOD **HOME USE**	2	3
4	5	6

ALL BOOKS MAY BE RECALLED AFTER 7 DAYS
1-month loans may be renewed by calling 642-3405
6-month loans may be recharged by bringing books to Circulation Desk
Renewals and recharges may be made 4 days prior to due date

DUE AS STAMPED BELOW

APR 5 1986
RECEIVED BY

MAR 27 1986

CIRCULATION DEPT.

UNIVERSITY OF CALIFORNIA, BERKELEY
FORM NO. DD6, 60m, 3/80   BERKELEY, CA 94720

Made in the USA
San Bernardino, CA
17 April 2014